© Copyright 2019 by Leslie Collins - All rights reserved

This document is geared towards providing exact and reliable information in regards to the topic and issue covered. The publication is sold with the idea that the publisher is not required to render accounting, officially permitted, or otherwise, qualified services. If advice is necessary, legal or professional, a practiced individual in the profession should be ordered.

Under no circumstance will any legal responsibility or blame be held against the publisher for any reparation, damages, or monetary loss due to the information herein, either directly or indirectly.

Legal Notice:

The book is copyright protected. This is only for personal use. You cannot amend, distribute, sell, use, quote or paraphrase any part or the content within this book without the consent of the author.

Disclaimer Notice:

Please note the information contained within this document is for educational and entertainment purposes only. Every attempt has been made to provide accurate, up to date and reliable complete information. No warranties of any kind are expressed or implied. Readers acknowledge that the author is not engaging in the rendering of legal, financial, medical or professional advice. The content of this book has been derived from various sources. Please consult a licensed professional before attempting any techniques outlined in this book.

By reading this document, the reader agrees that under no circumstances are is the author responsible for any loses, direct or indirect, which are incurred as a result the use of information contained within this document, including, but not limited to, ―errors, omissions, or inaccuracies.

Table of Contents

Introduction: An Overview Of The Ketogenic Diet 9

    What Can You Eat? 9

    What You Can't Eat 12

Chapter 1: How The Keto Diet Works 15

    Entering Ketosis 15

    Measuring Your Ketones 15

    Understanding Your Ketone Levels 16

Chapter 2: Benefits Of The Keto Diet 17

    Cutting Out Sugar and Carbs Makes Weight Loss Easier 17

    You'll Have More Energy 17

    You'll Experience Long-Term Relief From Inflammation 17

    Food Is More Satisfying 18

Chapter 3: How To Get Started On The Keto Diet 19

    Do: Cut the Worst Carbs Out Your Diet First 19

    Do: Prepare for "the Keto Flu" 19

    Do: Try Some Light Exercise 20

    Don't: Ignore Your Macros 20

    Don't: Skimp On Protein 20

    Don't: Obsess Over Your Ketone Levels 20

Chapter 4: 28 Days Keto Diet Meal Plan 21

Recipes Of Week ONE 21

DAY ONE 21

Avocado Deviled Eggs 21

Chicken Pasta 22

Stuffed cabbage casserole 24

DAY TWO 26

Cauliflower Grilled Cheese Sandwiches 26

Yellow Pepper Soup 28

Miso Salmon with Garlic powder 29

DAY THREE 30

Porridge 30

Smoke Salmon with Avocado 31

Fried Cauliflower rice 32

DAY FOUR 33

Blueberry Muffins 33

Keto club salad 34

Lemon Fish 35

DAY FIVE 36

Chocolate Chia Pudding 36

Spaghetti Squash Lasagna 37

Sweet and Sour meatballs 39

DAY SIX 40

Egg cups 40

Pork Salad 41

Cauliflower pizza 43

DAY SEVEN 44

Low-Carb Pancake 44

Crustless Kale Quiche 45

Tuna Casserole 46

Recipes Of Week TWO 47

DAY EIGHT 47

Easy Parmesan Zucchini Fries 47

Salad Niçoise 48

Beef Casserole 50

DAY NINE 51

Coconut pancake 51

Lemon Garlic Salmon with Asparagus 52

Chicken burgers with tomato butter 53

DAY TEN 55

Salmon filed avocado 55

Chicken Stew 56

Tuna salad with poached eggs 57

DAY ELEVEN 58

Chia pudding 58

Pork Chops 59

Caesar Salad 60

DAY TWELVE 61

Seafood Omelet 61

Tofu Chicken Curry 62

Kale with Beef and cranberries 64

DAY THIRTEEN 65

Avocado Smoothie 65

Salmon With Pesto And Spinach 66

Sausage & Pepper Soup 67

DAY FOURTEEN 68

Fluffy Buttermilk Pancakes 68

Crispy Fried Chicken 69

Kale Salad 70

Recipes Of Week THREE 71

DAY FIFTEEN 71

Sausage Breakfast Sandwich 71

Ground Beef Stir-Fry 72

Brussels sprouts with parmesan cheese 73

DAY SIXTEEN 74

Kale And Cheddar Scrambled Eggs 74

Stir Fried Pork with Cabbage Noodles 75

Spicy fish with butter-fried tomatoes 77

DAY SEVENTEEN 78

Pumpkin Pancake 78

Grilled Chicken and Spinach Pizza 79

Wrap with tuna and egg 81

DAY EIGHTEEN 83

Strawberry Crunch Smoothie 83

Easy Zucchini Beef Saute with Garlic and Cilantro 84

Cauliflower Tabbouleh with Halloumi cheese 85

DAY NINETEEN 87

Jalapeño Popper Egg Cups 87

Grilled Chicken Drumsticks with Garlic Marinade 88

Zucchini Pasta Pesto 89

DAY TWENTY 90

Brussels Sprouts Hash 90

Thai Beef Satay 91

Shrimp Chow Mein 92

DAY TWENTY ONE 93

Zucchini Egg Cups 93

Salmon Cakes 94

Green Beans Stir-Fry Recipe 95

Recipes Of Week Week-4 96

DAY TWENTY TWO ... 96

Lemon Cupcakes ... 96

Dill Pickle Soup ... 97

Corndogs ... 98

DAY TWENTY THREE ... 99

Tuna Poke Avocado Boats ... 99

Eggplant gratin ... 100

Chicken casserole with feta cheese and olives ... 101

DAY TWENTY FOUR ... 102

Fried Mac & Cheese with Rosemary ... 102

Chicken & Bacon Bites with Green Onion & Sage ... 103

Tuna Salad with Capers ... 104

DAY TWENTY FIVE ... 105

Coconut Peanut Balls ... 105

Chicken Wings with Creamy Broccoli ... 106

Salmon with Pesto ... 107

DAY TWENTY SIX ... 108

Chicken Cucumber Roll-Ups ... 108

Thai fish with Curry and Coconut ... 109

Greek salad ... 110

DAY TWENTY SEVEN ... 111

Brownies ... 111

Cheese Meatballs 112

Roasted fennel and snow pea salad 113

DAY TWENTY EIGHT 114

Asparagus Fries with Red Pepper Aioli 114

Paprika Chicken with Rutabaga 116

Red Coleslaw 117

Week1 118

Week-2 119

Week-3 120

Week-4 121

Introduction: An Overview Of The Ketogenic Diet

The Ketogenic diet is a low-carb, high-fat diet that emphasizes the good fats found in dairy, protein, seeds, and nuts. It's considered a "restrictive" diet because it eliminates grains, beans, and certain oils, vegetables, and fruit. It's one of the oldest diets with origins as far back as ancient Greece. The Keto diet as we know it was designed in the 1920's as a way to treat epilepsy. Before then, patients would refrain from all food, and their seizures stopped.

However, fasting isn't the most ideal long-term treatment, and medications were known for their mind-numbing properties. A low-carb, high-fat diet mimics many effects of fasting, but lets a patient eat good food and retain their cognitive abilities.

What Can You Eat?

The Keto diet includes meat, vegetables, fruit, seeds, and nuts. Quality is very important, so choose grass-fed meat, pasture-raised eggs, and wild-caught seafood. Organic veggies and fruit are also recommended to get the most benefits out of the diet. You are also allowed to eat dairy, but only if it's full-fat. The one exception is cow's milk, because it's too full of sugar. Instead, you can drink unsweetened nut milks.

Here is a list of food choices that are Keto-approved:

Proteins
Beef
Pork
Poultry
Eggs
Fish/seafood

Wild game

Full-fat dairy
Cheese
Cream cheese
Heavy cream
Greek yogurt

Low-carb vegetables
Cucumber
Bell peppers
Broccoli
Dark leafy greens
Tomatoes
Zucchini
Cauliflower
Garlic
Radishes
Sea vegetables

Low-carb fruits
Avocados
Berries
Lemons
Limes
Oranges

Nuts/seeds
Pecans

Macadamia nuts
Brazil nuts
Almonds
Hazelnuts
Walnuts
Chia seeds
Hemp seeds
Pumpkin seeds
Sunflower seeds
Flax seeds
Sesame seeds

Healthy fats/oils
Nut butters
Cocoa butter
Coconut cream
Coconut oil
Extra virgin olive oil
Ghee
Duck fat

Beverages
Water
Unsweetened herbal teas
Sparkling water
Unsweetened coffee
Unsweetened coconut water

What You Can't Eat

Anything that's high in carbs, sugar, and low in nutrition is not allowed on the Keto diet. There are some foods like vegetables relatively high in carbs that are okay in moderation, but they can hinder your progress, so they're really not recommended. All grains, low-fat, and artificial foods are not allowed at all. Here's a list of what you shouldn't eat while on the Keto diet:

Grains
Rice
Wheat
Corn
Quinoa
Buckwheat
Barley
Oatmeal
Cereals

Processed meat
Sausages
Grain-fed meats
Deli meat
Hot dogs

Certain oils
Corn
Sunflower
Canola/vegetable
Sesame

Grapeseed
Soybean
Peanut

Beans/legumes
Kidney
Black
Fava
White
Chickpeas
Green peas
Lentils

Low-fat/fat-free dairy products
Butter substitutes
Skim milk
Low-fat "diet" ice cream
Low-fat/fat-free yogurt

High-carb vegetables
Sweet potatoes
Squash
Artichokes
Corn
White potatoes
Yams

High-sugar fruits
Bananas

Apples
Mangoes
Grapes
Dried fruit

Refined sweeteners
Corn syrup
Maple syrup
Raw sugar
Cane sugar
White sugar
Agave nectar

Artificial sweeteners
Aspartame
Saccharin
Splenda
Equal

Junk food
Baked goods
Fast food
Ice cream
Candy
Alcohol
"Diet" food

Chapter 1: How The Keto Diet Works

There's a very specific scientific process behind the Keto diet. To understand it, let's go over what happens when the body uses carb, its usual source of fuel. You eat carbs and the body turns them into glucose. The small intestine absorbs this glucose and carries it to the liver, which is responsible for dispersing it to your cells for energy. Extra glucose is stored as fat. The average diet is very high in carbs, which explains why many people are overweight.

Entering Ketosis

On the Keto diet, you eliminate most of the carbs the body would use as fuel and replace them with fat. To use this fat as energy, the body needs to transform it into a substance it can use. During this process, compounds known as "ketones" are created, thus the name "the Ketogenic diet." The body doesn't begin to create ketones unless you're eating a certain amount of fat, specifically, around 60-75% of your daily calories. 15-30% come from protein and the final 5-10% come from carbs. It's impossible to cut *all* carbs from your diet, so you should aim to limit your intake to 20 net grams per day.

Measuring Your Ketones

How do you know if you're in ketosis? You can actually measure your body's ketone levels. It's especially important to do this on a regular basis if you're diabetic because too many ketones can be life-threatening. Ketones make the blood acidic and that acidity is very bad for diabetics. There are three ways to measure ketones:

A blood meter

This test measures the BHB ketone (beta-hydroxybutyrate).

A urine strip

Cheaper, but slightly-less accurate than a blood meter, a urine strip measures levels of the acetoacetate ketone. It's best to use this test when you're first starting out, because once you've been in ketosis for a while, your acetoacetate levels don't register.

A breath test

Breath tests measure acetone, which tends to follow the levels of BHB, so it's a good way to get an idea of where both these ketones are in your system. These tests are initially more expensive than urine strips, but they're reusable.

Understanding Your Ketone Levels

Your ketone levels are measured in mmol/L, or millimole per liter. The levels you want depend on your goals. If you're hoping to lose weight on the Keto diet, your levels should be above 0.5 mmol/L. For sharper mental abilities, aim for 1.5-3 mmol/L, while symptoms of mental illness should improve around 3.6 mmol/L, but you really don't want to be any higher. For better athletic performance, anything above 0.5 mmol/L should help.

Bear in mind these levels do not apply if you're diabetic. Your levels will need to be much lower if you want to be safe. When you start getting between 0.6-1.5 mmol/L, you should talk to your doctor about lowering your ketones. 1.6 mmol/L puts you at risk for ketoacidosis, which is acidic blood. If you ever get as high as 3 mmol/L, you need to go to the emergency room. At this point, you'll likely be vomiting and feeling ill, so know that high ketone levels are the reason.

Chapter 2: Benefits Of The Keto Diet

There are a lot of reasons to avoid carbs and embrace fat. The Keto diet has mostly been studied on those with epilepsy, but there are benefits for everyone. If you've been struggling to lose weight and/or experiencing fatigue, joint pain, and "brain fog," here's why you should consider the Keto diet:

Cutting Out Sugar and Carbs Makes Weight Loss Easier

In the not-so distant past, experts told us that fat was the enemy. We were told to eat low-fat and fat-free food, but the reality is that sugar is actually the real problem. It's sugar that causes obesity and a host of other health problems. By cutting out sugar and refined carbs, which the body uses the same as glucose, you have a much better chance of dropping extra weight and getting healthier.

You'll Have More Energy

When you eat a meal like pasta, don't you just want to take a nap? A diet heavy in carbs can cause fatigue and a "heavy" feeling in your body and mind. When you replace those carbs with fat, you'll gain a lot more energy. Foods like avocados and coconut oil are known for their energy-boosting qualities and positive effect on the brain, so you'll feel better prepared to handle long days and hard workouts. Cutting out sugar will also have a significant impact on your energy, since sugar causes your blood sugar to spike and crash. Eating a balance of healthy fat and protein keeps those levels even.

You'll Experience Long-Term Relief From Inflammation

Inflammation is behind a lot of the pain our bodies experience. You're probably familiar with aching joint pain, stiffness, and muscle fatigue. Inflammation can also cause flu-like symptoms. An unhealthy diet high in sugar causes inflammation throughout the body. When you cut out sugar, your body is finally able to heal. Healthy fats and protein also encourage cell growth, which repairs inflammation damage, so the Keto diet treats every aspect of the problem.

Food Is More Satisfying

When you eat a lot of simple, refined carbs like bread and pasta, your body burns them up quickly. That's why you feel hungry so soon after meals high in that type of food. The same goes for sugary foods, which can be as addicting as a drug. The Keto diet is full of foods that satisfy you for hours to come. That's because the few carbs you do eat burn much more slowly, and Keto-approved foods tend to be high in fiber. The body is able to use its fuel much more efficiently rather than burning it up in a quick flash.

Chapter 3: How To Get Started On The Keto Diet

Starting a new diet is always hard, and when it's as restrictive as the Keto diet, it can seem really overwhelming. There are a few tips you can follow that make the transition much easier. Knowing the most common mistakes is also helpful because you know what *not* to do. Here are six pieces of advice - three "do's" and three "don'ts" - that can make a huge difference.

Do: Cut the Worst Carbs Out Your Diet First

Eliminating nearly all carbs from your diet can be a really big challenge for a lot of people. Many try to go all-in right away and get discouraged quickly. To ease yourself into the Keto diet, consider a more gradual approach by getting rid of the *worst* carbs first. This includes sugary junk food like candy, fast food, ice cream, and baked goods. Don't worry about the higher-carb vegetables and fruit when you're getting started. Once you've eliminated the worst carb offenders, you can start to get more restrictive.

Do: Prepare for "the Keto Flu"

Also known as the low-carb flu, this is a common experience for people when they start aiming for ketosis. As your body switches from carbs to fat, some flu-like symptoms can arise, like headaches, fatigue, and even nausea. Anticipate these issues and prepare by staying extra hydrated, drinking chicken broth that you salt yourself, and eating slow-burning carbs like grapes or squash. Keep in mind that the keto flu should never make you feel so sick that it disrupts your life. If you start vomiting, go see your doctor.

Do: Try Some Light Exercise

When you're starting on the Keto diet, exercise may be the last thing you want to think about. However, it actually encourages your body's transition into ketosis. Why? Exercise lets the body burn the few carbs you're eating first, forcing it to use the fat from your diet and produce ketones. Since you'll likely feel fatigued when you start Keto, keep the exercise light. Yoga and pilates are good, as well as anything that gets your heart rate up.

Don't: Ignore Your Macros

While you don't count calories on the Keto diet, the percentage of fat to protein and carbs is very important. If you ignore it, you'll find it difficult to enter ketosis. You can find the number of grams best for your specific needs by using a keto calculator, like one on the website ruled.me. It has you put in your age, weight, height, activity level, and goals.

Don't: Skimp On Protein

The Keto diet isn't a high-protein diet, but you still want to be aware of how much you're getting. If you want to lose weight, getting enough protein is especially important since it causes your body to release glucagon, a compound that makes you feel satisfied after eating.

Don't: Obsess Over Your Ketone Levels

Being in ketosis is obviously the point of the Keto diet, true, but your specific ketone levels aren't necessarily the most important factor. As we mentioned earlier, 3.6 mmol/L is the highest anyone should be, and there's even debate about whether benefits increase after just 3.0 mmol/L. Your ketone tests will also eventually stop showing high ketone levels because your body is using them up. As long as you're between 0.5 and 3.0 mmol/L, you're good. Pay closer attention to how you feel health and energy-wise as a way to measure your progress.

Chapter 4: 28 Days Keto Diet Meal Plan

Recipes Of Week ONE
DAY ONE
Avocado Deviled Eggs

Serves: 3

Cooking Time: 00 minutes

Preparation Time: 05 minutes

Ingredients

- 6 cooked eggs
- 1 large avocado, peeled and seed removed
- 1/2 cup low crab mayonnaise
- 2 tablespoons lime juice
- 1teaspoon salt or to taste
- freshly ground black pepper
- 4 tablespoons chives

Instructions:

1) Halve the avocado and remove the seed . Halve the eggs and carefully without breaking the egg whites - put the egg yolk in a bowl.
2) Place the chopped avocado in a food processor and add egg yolk, mayonnaise, lime juice, salt and pepper. Process until smooth. Alternatively, crush with a fork until creamy and well mixed.
3) Fill the egg whites and make stuffed eggs

Nutrition information According to Keto Diet

Calories per serving: 147 ; Carbohydrates: 1.1 g; Protein: 2.2 g; Fat: 14.8 g

Chicken Pasta

Serves: 4

Cooking Time: 35 minutes

Preparation Time: 10 minutes

Ingredients

- 4 chicken breasts
- 3 tablespoons coconut oil
- Salt and pepper to taste
- 20 cherry tomatoes
- 4medium Yellow squash
- Fresh basil for garnish
- For the pesto:
- 2 cups basil
- 1/2 cup Pecans
- 2 cloves garlic
- 1 lemon, zest and juice
- 1/2cup grated Parmesan
- 1/2 cup coconut oil
- 1 teaspoon salt

Instructions:

1) Preheat the oven to 400 ° F. Place the chicken breast on a baking tray, sprinkle with 1 tablespoon coconut oil and season with salt and crushed black pepper. Bake for 15 minutes.

2) Remove the chicken from the oven to add tomatoes , again brush with coconut oil . Return to the oven and cook for another 15 minutes or until the chicken is lightly browned and cooked.

3) In the meantime, prepare the pesto by mixing all ingredients except coconut oil. Once a paste has formed, slowly add the oil while the blender is running and stop it as soon as the pesto is well combined to achieve the desired consistency.
4) To make your pasta, spiral yellow squash or use a vegetable peeler to make Yellow squash ribbons.
5) In a saucepan with 1 tablespoon of coconut oil, saute yellow squash for 3 minutes or until tender. Remove from heat and stir in pesto.
6) Mount the plate by placing half of the yellow squash pesto in each bowl. Garnish with chopped chicken, baked tomatoes and fresh basil.

Nutrition information According to Keto Diet

Calories per serving: 891.5 ; Carbohydrates: 10.59 g; Protein: 70.68 g; Fat: 61.79 g

Stuffed cabbage casserole

Serves: 2

Cooking Time: 30 minutes

Preparation Time: 10 minutes

Ingredients

- ¾ lb green cabbage
- 1/2 cup grass-fed- butter
- 8 oz. ground pork
- ½ teaspoon salt
- ½ teaspoon onion powder
- 1/8 teaspoon ground black pepper
- 1 tablespoon Tex-Mex seasoning
- ½ tablespoon white wine vinegar
- 1/4 cup shredded cheese, preferably cheddar cheese
- 2 oz. leafy greens or lettuce

Instructions:

1) Preheat the oven to 400 °F. Shred the cabbage with a sharp knife or in a food processor.
2) Fry the cabbage in 1 tablespoon of butter in a large pan or wok over medium heat. Fry until smooth, but do not let cabbage turn brown. It may take a little longer. about 10 minutes.
3) Add spices and vinegar. Stir and cook for a few more minutes. Set aside on a plate.
4) Melt the remaining butter in the same pan. Fry the minced meat and fry it over medium heat until most of the juices have evaporated. Lower the heat to medium-low.
5) Add the fried cabbage and sauté for a minute with the meat. Remove from heat and season with salt and pepper.
6) Stir the cheese into the cabbage mixture and place in a casserole dish.

7) Sprinkle on the remaining cheese and bake for 15 to 20 minutes or until the cheese turns brown.

8) Serve with a green salad.

Nutrition information According to Keto Diet

Calories per serving: 831; Carbohydrates: 9 g; Protein: 44 g; Fat: 67 g

DAY TWO
Cauliflower Grilled Cheese Sandwiches

Serves: 8

Cooking Time: 15 minutes

Preparation Time: 10 minutes

Ingredients

- 2 head cauliflower
- 2 eggs beaten
- 3 cups Edam cheese grated
- 24 slices mozzarella Cheese
- 1/4 teaspoon dried sage
- 1/4 teaspoon dried oregano
- ground black pepper
- Grass-fed- butter for greasing
- fresh parsley for garnishing

Instructions:

1) Place grated or finely chopped cauliflower in a covered microwave dish. Microwave about 5 minutes or until just tender.
2) Filter the excess liquid from cooked cauliflower rice.
3) Put the cauliflower, the beaten egg and 1 cup of grated cheese in a bowl and sprinkle with pepper, , sage and oregano . Mix well.
4) In a slightly greased baking sheet, form cauliflower mixture resembling a slice of bread. This recipe made 8 slices, about ½ inch thick for each slice. More slices for thinner pieces
5) Cook the cauliflower slices in an oven preheated to 350 ° C for about 10 to 12 minutes.
6) In a pan butter melts on low heat and put a slice of "bread" cauliflower, cover with slices of mozzarella cheese, grated cheese, covered with slices of mozzarella cheese and top with another piece of "Pan" cauliflower

7) Cover the pan and watch as the mozzarella cheese melts on low heat. Occasionally check the underside to avoid burns. If the heat is not loud enough, switch to medium heat, but move the "bread" cauliflower cheese on the sides and then cover the pan again.
8) Turn to the other side and continue to melt the mozzarella cheese. Edam cheese does not melt quickly, it mixes with melted mozzarella cheese. Use a large, multi-sized pair of tongs to safely return the cauliflower sandwich. I used a wide, wide and wide tongs with several portions to bring back the sandwich safely.
9) Once the mozzarella has melted to the desired consistency, put on a plate, garnish with parsley and enjoy!

Nutrition information According to Keto Diet

Calories per serving: 503; Carbohydrates: 9 g; Protein: 33 g; Fat: 37 g

Yellow Pepper Soup

Serves: 2

Cooking Time: 40 minutes

Preparation Time: 10 minutes

Ingredients

- 2 whole roasted yellow peppers
- 1/8 cup chopped onion
- 1/2 teaspoon chilli pepper flakes
- 1/2 teaspoon minced garlic
- 1/2 cup heavy whipping cream
- 1/4 cup grass-fed-butter
- Salt and pepper to taste
- 2 tablespoons Parmesan cheese

Instructions:

1) Mix both the whole peppers in a blender without water, and puree until it becomes a thick sauce.
2) Add the onions, salt, pepper and chili flakes and puree.
3) Heat your teaspoon of garlic in a saucepan.
4) Add the pepper / chilli mixture and bring to a boil.
5) Beat in the cream and bring to the boil again.
6) Quickly pour the butter into the soup. Stir and the soup should start to get thicker.
7) Bring to a boil.
8) Serve and garnish with some Parmesan!

Nutrition information According to Keto Diet

Calories per serving: 385.75; Carbohydrates: 4 g; Protein: 7.57 g; Fat: 36.8 g

Miso Salmon with Garlic powder

Serves: 2

Cooking Time: 25 minutes

Preparation Time: 30 minutes

Ingredients

- 1 pounds salmon fillets with skin
- Kosher salt to taste
- 1 tablespoon garlic powder
- tablespoons white wine
- 1-1/2 tablespoons miso, white miso preferred

Instructions:

1) Cut the salmon into fillets..
2) Sprinkle the kosher salt and garlic powder over the fillets and let stand for 30 minutes. This will extract some of the moisture.
3) Mix white wine and 1-1/2 tablespoons of miso in a bowl.
4) Pour about 1/3 of the marinade into the bottom of an airtight container. Put the steaks in the bowl and pour the remainder of the marinade over it. Put the lid on and keep it in the fridge for 1-2 days.
5) When baking, preheat the oven to 400 ° F. Use a piece of parchment paper on a baking sheet or a well-oiled one. The parchment paper will not stick the salmon, so try it if you can. Cook the salmon for 25 minutes.

Nutrition information According to Keto Diet

Calories per serving: 215.25; Carbohydrates: 0.78 g; Protein: 28.38 g; Fat: 9.23 g

DAY THREE
Porridge

Serves: 2

Cooking Time: 05 minutes

Preparation Time: 05 minutes

Ingredients

- 4 tablespoons Almond flour
- 6 tablespoons golden flaxseed meal
- 4 tablespoons vanilla protein powder
- 3 cups unsweetened almond milk
- Stevia to taste

Instructions:

1) Mix Almond flour, golden flaxseed meal and vanilla protein powder in a bowl.
2) Put the almond milk in a saucepan and cook over medium heat. In the beginning it will look very relaxed.
3) When it gets thicker, you can add your favorite amount of sweetener.. Serve with your favorite topping like berries,etc

Nutrition information According to Keto Diet

Calories per serving: 249; Carbohydrates: 5.78 g; Protein: 17 g; Fat: 13 g

Smoke Salmon with Avocado

Serves: 2

Cooking Time: 05 minutes

Preparation Time: 05 minutes

Ingredients

- 0.88 lb smoked salmon
- 4 avocados
- 1/2 cup low crab mayonnaise
- salt and pepper

Instructions:

1) Halve the avocado, remove the pit and scoop the avocado pieces with a spoon. Put it on a plate.
2) Add salmon and a generous spoonful of mayonnaise to the plate.
3) Garnish with freshly ground black pepper and a pinch of sea salt.

Nutrition information According to Keto Diet

Calories per serving: 250; Carbohydrates: 7.8 g; Protein: 13.2 g; Fat: 19.3 g

Fried Cauliflower rice

Serves: 6

Cooking Time: 05 minutes

Preparation Time: 05 minutes

Ingredients

- 2 small head of cauliflower, cut into florets
- 4 large eggs
- 2 onion, sliced thin
- 2 tablespoons avocado oil
- 1 tablespoon fish sauce
- 1 tablespoon soy sauce
- 1 teaspoon freshly ground black pepper
- 1 teaspoon garlic, minced
- 1 teaspoon ginger, minced

Instructions:

1) Cauliflower rice flowers in food processor.
2) Add the avocado oil to the pan and fry the cauliflower.
3) After a few minutes, squeeze your cauliflower to the side of the pan and add the garlic, ginger and onions to the empty side.
4) Add fish sauce, soy sauce and black pepper to "rice".
5) Mix everything and fry for a few minutes.
6) Put all your ingredients back on the side of the pan. Add your eggs and let them cook.
7) Mix well and serve

Nutrition information According to Keto Diet

Calories per serving: 214.33; Carbohydrates: 5.27 g; Protein: 11.5 g; Fat: 16.11 g

DAY FOUR
Blueberry Muffins

Serves: 6

Cooking Time: 20 minutes

Preparation Time: 10 minutes

Ingredients

- 2 cups coconut flour
- 10 drops Stevia
- 1 cup Buttermilk
- 1/3 cup Coconut oil
- 1/2 cup coconut milk
- 2 large Egg
- 1/4 teaspoon Vanilla extract
- 3/4 cup Blueberries

Instructions:

1) Preheat the oven to 350 degrees F. Align a muffin tin with 6 silicone paper or parchment cupcake liners.
2) In a large bowl, mix coconut flour, Stevia and buttermilk.
3) Mix the melted coconut oil, coconut milk, eggs and vanilla extract. Fold the blueberries.
4) Evenly distribute the mixture between the muffin pans. Bake for about 20 minutes until the top is golden and an inserted toothpick comes out clean.

Nutrition information According to Keto Diet

Calories per serving: 217; Carbohydrates: 3 g; Protein: 7 g; Fat: 19g

Keto club salad

Serves: 6

Cooking Time: 20 minutes

Preparation Time: 10 minutes

Ingredients

- 6 cups romaine lettuce, torn into pieces
- 1 cup cherry tomatoes, halved
- 2 cups diced English cucumber
- 4 tablespoons sour cream
- 2 tablespoons low crab mayonnaise
- 1 teaspoon garlic mined
- 1 teaspoon onion powder
- 2 teaspoons dried parsley
- 2 tablespoon almond milk
- 6 large hard boiled eggs, sliced
- 4 ounces cheddar cheese, cubed

Instructions:

1) Prepare the vinaigrette by mixing sour cream, mayonnaise and dried herbs until combined.
2) Add a spoonful of almond milk and mix. If the dressing appears too thick, add another spoonful of almond milk. Do not forget to add another spoon of milk to the final fat / protein / carbohydrate count if you do!
3) Cover the salad with fresh vegetables, cheese and sliced eggs. Drizzle with prepared vinaigrette, about 2 tablespoons per serving, then stir to cover

Nutrition information According to Keto Diet

Calories per serving: 329.67; Carbohydrates: 4.83 g; Protein: 16.82 g; Fat: 26.32g

Lemon Fish

Serves: 4

Cooking Time: 20 minutes

Preparation Time: 10 minutes

Ingredients

- 14 ounces fresh fish fillets
- 6 tablespoons coconut oil
- 2 tablespoons lemon juice
- 1/2 cup fine coconut flour
- 2 teaspoons dill
- 2 teaspoons dried basil
- 2 teaspoons onion powder
- 1 teaspoon garlic mined
- Salt and pepper to taste

Instructions:

1) In a large bowl, mix coconut flour, dill, basil, onion powder, minced garlic, salt and pepper and mix evenly.
2) Take the fresh fish fillets in turn and squeeze in the flour mixture. Turn and repeat. You want to cover them really well and then put them in a separate dish. You can do it in advance and keep it in the fridge until cooked.
3) Heat half of the coconut oil and half of the lemon juice pan over medium heat. You want it hot enough to crust the flour mix but we don't want to burn the butter or turn the juice bitter.
4) Let the fish cook for about 3 minutes. Give the pan a touch so that the fish absorbs all the oil with lemon juice.
5) Put the other half of the oil and the remaining lemon juice in the pan and turn the fish for 3 minutes. Turn the pan again and fish a bit. The coating should be beautiful and golden, and you should be able to see how the fish is cooked.
6) Make sure the fish is done with a fork and remove it from the pan when it's almost done. Makes a nice dressing.

Nutrition information According to Keto Diet

Calories per serving: 406; Carbohydrates: 3.55 g; Protein: 29.07 g; Fat: 30.33g

DAY FIVE
Chocolate Chia Pudding

Serves: 4

Cooking Time: 00 minutes

Preparation Time: 05 minutes

Ingredients

- 4 teaspoons unsweetened cacao powder
- 1 teaspoon nutmeg powder
- 4 tablespoons chia seeds
- 1 cup almond milk
- 1/4 teaspoon vanilla extract
- Stevia to taste

Instructions:

1) In a mixer pour almond milk, cocoa powder, vanilla extract, Stevia and nutmeg powder mix
2) Mix until smooth
3) Transfer the mixture to a quarter of a glass
4) Add the chia seeds and shake well
5) Cool overnight so that the chia seeds soften and absorb the fluid
6) serve

Nutrition information According to Keto Diet

Calories per serving: 77; Carbohydrates: 3 g; Protein: 6 g; Fat: 5g

Spaghetti Squash Lasagna

Serves: 5

Cooking Time: 1 hr. 30 minutes

Preparation Time: 15 minutes

Ingredients

- 1/2 whole spaghetti squash
- 1 tablespoons Avocado oil, divided
- 1/4 medium onion, diced
- 1/2 pound ground pork
- 1/2 tablespoon garlic powder
- 12 Oz marinara sauce
- 10 Oz whole milk ricotta
- 1 large egg
- 3/2 cup grated Parmesan cheese, divided
- 1 tablespoons chopped parsley
- 1/4 teaspoon salt
- 1/4 teaspoon pepper
- 4 ounces sliced mozzarella cheese

Instructions:

1. Preheat the oven to 400 ° F.
2. Carefully halve and core the spaghetti squash in the middle. Sprinkle with 1 tablespoon of Avocado oil and sprinkle with salt and pepper.
3. Grill for 35-45 minutes or until squash is tender and easily shreds with a fork. Remove from the skin in a bowl and set aside
4. While you are roasting the squash , heat the remaining tablespoon of Avocado oil in a large pan. Add chopped onion, minced meat and garlic powder.
5. Cook the meat thoroughly and drain the melted fat.

6. Add the marinara sauce to the meat mixture and bring to a boil. Reduce heat and simmer sauce for about 15 minutes or until thickened and most of the liquid is reduced.
7. While simmering, place the ricotta, 1/4 cup Parmesan, eggs, basil and ½ teaspoon salt and pepper in a medium bowl and set aside.
8. Lower the oven to 350 ° F and lightly grease a 2.5 liter casserole.
9. Start with the spaghetti squash, add half the shreds (about 1 cup) to the bottom of the bowl and press a flat layer.
10. Garnish with half of the ricotta mix, then half of the meat sauce and half of the mozzarella.
11. Repeat the layers again, starting with another layer of sqush.
12. Sprinkle pan with 1/4 cup of Parmesan and chopped parsley.
13. Cover with aluminum foil and bake for 30 minutes. Remove the aluminum foil and bake for 20 to 30 minutes or until the mixture is bubbly and golden. Leave at least 15 minutes before serving.

Nutrition information According to Keto Diet

Calories per serving: 577.7; Carbohydrates: 10.29 g; Protein: 30.16 g; Fat: 45.58g

Sweet and Sour meatballs

Serves: 2

Cooking Time: 20 minutes

Preparation Time: 05 minutes

Ingredients

The meatballs:

- 1/2 pound ground pork
- 1 large egg
- 1/8 cup Parmesan cheese
- 1/4 cup onion minced

For the sauce:

- 1 cup water
- 1/8 cup apple cider vinegar
- 1-1/2 tablespoons soy sauce
- 1/2 cup tomato puree
- 1 cup erythritol

Instructions:

1) In a large bowl Add ground Pork, egg, grated Parmesan cheese and onion. Mix with your hands.
2) Then use a measuring spoon to shape the meatballs. You should be able to make 15 mini meatballs.
3) Preheat a pot over medium heat. Add the meatballs and cook until golden brown. If it's a bit pink in the middle, it's good now. Put aside.
4) Add water, apple cider vinegar, soy sauce, tomato puree and erythritol to the same pan. Stir with a whisk until the sauce comes together.
5) After a few minutes, check the sauce to make sure it's the desired consistency.
6) Add the meatballs and simmer for 10 minutes or until the meatballs are cooked through.

Nutrition information According to Keto Diet

Calories per serving: 295.4; Carbohydrates: 5.35 g; Protein: 28.26 g; Fat:18.66g

DAY SIX

Egg cups

Serves: 2

Cooking Time: 25 minutes

Preparation Time: 05 minutes

Ingredients

- 2 ounces cheddar cheese
- 1 ounces cream cheese
- 2 medium Cayenne chiles, de-seeded and chopped
- 6 strips bacon
- 4 large eggs
- 1/4 teaspoon minced garlic
- 1/4 cup chopped onion
- Salt and pepper to taste

Instructions:

1) Preheat the oven to 375F. pre-cook Bacon, so half crispy, but still flexible. Add the bacon grease to the mixture.
2) Mix all ingredients with a hand blender (except cheddar and 1 Cayenne).
3) Grass the muffin tin and place the pre-cooked bacon on the edges.
4) Add the egg mixture to the muffin tin. Do not overfill.
5) Add the cheddar cheese on top of the muffins tin, then a Cayenne ring. Bake at 375F for 20-25 minutes.
6) After cooking, remove from the oven to cool.

Nutrition information According to Keto Diet

Calories per serving: 157.17; Carbohydrates: 1.35 g; Protein: 9.75 g; Fat:12.28g

Pork Salad

Serves: 4

Cooking Time: 25 minutes

Preparation Time: 05 minutes

Ingredients

- 9 ounces pork belly slices
- 2 teaspoons salt
- 1/4 cup Almond
- 1 teaspoon water
- 1 tablespoon Erythritol
- 1.41 ounces Full-fat cheeses
- 1/4 cup Blueberry
- 1 teaspoon Dijon mustard
- 2 tablespoons white wine vinegar
- 2 teaspoons Avocado oil
- 4 ounces mixed greens

Instructions:

1) Set your oven to your broil setting.
2) Take your pork slices and cover with 1 teaspoon of Avocado oil and apply plenty of salt on both sides. Bake until golden and crispy. About 20-30 minutes.
3) While you wait for your pork to be cooked, cut the almonds halves into smaller pieces.
4) Heat a pan over medium heat and add water and Erythritol to the pan. Wait for the Erythritol to dissolve and add the roughly chopped nuts. cook for about 5 minutes, until the liquid in the nuts thickens and caramelizes.
5) Transfer your nuts into a tray to cool.
6) Cut the cheese into small pieces and set aside.

7) Prepare your vinaigrette with mustard, white wine vinegar and Avocado oil in a small bowl and whisk or mix with a fork until thick.

8) Remove the crispy pork from the oven and let cool and cut into small pieces.

9) Mix your salad leaves with the vinaigrette and cover with sliced pork belly, candied nuts, cheese and Blueberry.

Nutrition information According to Keto Diet

Calories per serving: 537; Carbohydrates: 4.77 g; Protein: 12.75 g; Fat:51.7g

Cauliflower pizza

Serves: 8

Cooking Time: 30 minutes

Preparation Time: 10 minutes

Ingredients

- 8 cups florets
- 2 cups parmesan cheese grated
- 1/4 cup onion minced
- 1/4 tsp garlic minced
- 2 eggs

Instructions:

1) Preheat the oven to 400 degrees Fahrenheit.
2) Put the cauliflower in a food processor and squeeze until it crumbles and looks like rice.
3) Heat the cauliflower rice in a dry pan over medium heat and often stir for about 10 minutes to remove as much moisture as possible. As soon as it appears a bit dry, add Parmesan and spices.
4) Continue cooking over medium heat until Parmesan is melted.
5) Remove from heat and add the eggs.
6) Use the parchment on a 12-inch round pizza pan and spray with cooking spray. Put another piece of parchment paper on top and spread the "dough" and smooth as much as you can. Make the edges slightly higher to form a crust.
7) Bake for 20 minutes. Add your favorite topping and cook for another 10 minutes. Cut into 16 large slices and serve!

Nutrition information According to Keto Diet

Calories per serving: 132; Carbohydrates: 4 g; Protein: 11 g; Fat:7g

DAY SEVEN

Low-Carb Pancake

Serves: 8

Cooking Time: 30 minutes

Preparation Time: 10 minutes

Ingredients

- 3 eggs
- 1/2 cup flax meal
- 1/2 cup Almond milk
- 1 tablespoon melted butter
- ½ pinch salt
- ½ teaspoon baking powder
- coconut oil for frying

Instructions:

1) Separate the egg yolks from the egg white and beat the egg whites and beat the salt with a hand mixer. Continue whisking until stiff peaks form and set aside.
2) In another bowl mix egg yolk, oil and almond milk.
3) Add flax meal and baking powder. Mix in a gentle mixture.
4) Always carefully fold the egg whites into the dough. Let the dough rest for 5 minutes.
5) Fry in coconut oil over medium or low heat for a few minutes on each side.

Nutrition information According to Keto Diet

Calories per serving: 291; Carbohydrates: 3 g; Protein: 12 g; Fat:24g

Crustless Kale Quiche

Serves: 2

Cooking Time: 30 minutes

Preparation Time: 10 minutes

Ingredients

- 3 eggs, lightly beaten
- 1 tablespoon coconut oil
- 1 teaspoon garlic powder,
- 1/4 red onion, diced
- 1/4 red pepper, diced
- 1/2 cup kale, chopped
- Salt and pepper, to taste
- Swiss cheese to top

Instructions:

1) Preheat the oven to 400 ° F.
2) In a large pan, heat the coconut oil and add the garlic powder and a pinch of sea salt. fry for a few minutes.
3) Add the onions and red pepper and sauté until lightly browned.
4) Add the kale and sauté for 5-10 minutes until lightly withered.
5) Lightly grease a pie pan with coconut oil.
6) Once the vegetables are ready, add them to the pie pan. Then add the beaten eggs and mix. Season with salt and pepper. Garnish with Swiss cheese for an extra boost.
7) Bake 25 to 30 minutes or until eggs are cooked. You can try to put a fork in the middle, and if there is no egg on the fork, you are good!

Nutrition information According to Keto Diet

Calories per serving: 402; Carbohydrates: 3.8 g; Protein: 19.4 g; Fat:33.9g

Tuna Casserole

Serves: 2

Cooking Time: 30 minutes

Preparation Time: 10 minutes

Ingredients

- 1/4 cup grass-fed- butter
- 1/2 onion
- 1/2 red bell pepper
- 1/2 cup Bok choy
- 1 cup tuna in olive oil, drained
- 1/2 cup mayonnaise
- 1/4 cup freshly shredded parmesan cheese
- 1 teaspoon chili flakes
- salt and pepper
- 1/2 cup baby spinach

Instructions:

1) Preheat the oven to 400 ° F .Finely chop the onion, pepper and Bok choy and fry in a large pan until lightly mixed. Season with salt and pepper.
2) Mix the tuna, mayonnaise, parmesan and chili in a greased casserole dish. Add the fried vegetables and stir.
3) Bake for 15 to 20 minutes or until golden brown.
4) Serve with young spinach

Nutrition information According to Keto Diet

Calories per serving: 953; Carbohydrates: 5 g; Protein: 43 g; Fat:83 g

Recipes Of Week TWO

DAY EIGHT

Easy Parmesan Zucchini Fries

Serves: 2

Cooking Time: 15 minutes

Preparation Time: 10 minutes

Ingredients

- 1 medium Zucchini
- 3/8 cup Grated parmesan cheese
- 1 large Egg
- 1/4 teaspoon Garlic minced
- 1/4 tsp Black pepper
- 1/4 cup Coconut flour

Instructions:

1) Preheat the oven to 400F.
2) Cut the zucchini into matchsticks, making sure each stick has some bark.
3) Add egg to a bowl and mix well.
4) Add the Parmesan, coconut flour and place in a second bowl.
5) Dip each piece of zucchini into the egg mixture, then mix the coconut flour mixer and place on a baking sheet.
6) Roast for 15-20 minutes until it begins to crack at the edges. Serves hot.

Nutrition information According to Keto Diet

Calories per serving: 131; Carbohydrates: 3 g; Protein: 11 g; Fat:8 g

Salad Niçoise

Serves: 4

Cooking Time: 10 minutes

Preparation Time: 15 minutes

Ingredients

- 4 eggs
- 1 cup beets
- 400 g fresh green beans
- 4 tablespoons coconut oil
- 1 teaspoon garlic powder
- 400 g Romaine lettuce
- 1/2 cup cherry tomatoes
- 1 red onion
- 2 cans tofu
- 10 olives
- salt and pepper

Dressing

- 1 tablespoon Dijon mustard
- 4 tablespoons small capers
- 1 tablespoon olive oil
- 1/4 cup mayonnaise
- 2 tablespoons fresh basil
- 1 lemon, the juice
- 1 teaspoon garlic powder

Instructions:

1) Mix all ingredients for the dressing with a blender and blend until they are complete and creamy. set aside .

2) Boil the eggs as you wish, soft or hard. Immediately place in ice-cold water when ready to peel more easily. Cut them into quarters.

3) Wash and peel the beets. Cut them into pieces of half an inch. Wash and cut the green beans and cook for 5 minutes in slightly salted water. Use separate pots Rinse with cold water when done.

4) Put a pan on medium heat and sauté the green beans in coconut oil. Add garlic powder . Season with salt and pepper.

5) Put the tofu on medium heat and saute

6) Put the salad on a plate . Add the tomatoes, onions, saute tofu, eggs, beans, olives and beets . Serve with a vinaigrette on the side.

Nutrition information According to Keto Diet

Calories per serving: 521; Carbohydrates: 6.5 g; Protein: 54.2 g; Fat:28.9 g

Beef Casserole

Serves:4

Cooking Time:25minutes

Preparation Time: 10 minutes

Ingredients

- 8 ounces broccoli rice
- 1 pound ground beef
- 8 ounces green enchilada sauce
- 1/4 cup sour cream
- 1 cup low fat yogurt
- 1 cup shredded cheddar cheese
- 1/4 cup sliced onions
- 1 teaspoon salt
- 1 teaspoon black pepper

Instructions:

1) Preheat the oven to 350 ° F. Place the broccoli rice in a microwaveable container and cook for 4-5 minutes until soft.
2) Fry the meat over medium heat. Pour Enchilada green sauce and season with salt and pepper.
3) Add the sour cream, yogurt and onions to the bowl with the cauliflower. Mix very well
4) Put the broccoli mixture in a casserole dish and distribute evenly.
5) Cover the broccoli with half of the meat mixture.
6) Sprinkle with 1 cup of grated cheddar cheese.
7) Make another layer with the remaining meat and another layer with the remaining cheddar cheese.
8) Bake for 20 minutes at 350 ° F.

Nutrition information According to Keto Diet

Calories per serving: 427.13; Carbohydrates: 5.74g; Protein: 33.26 g; Fat:28.79 g

DAY NINE
Coconut pancake

Serves: 2

Cooking Time: 15 minutes

Preparation Time: 15 minutes

Ingredients

- 3 eggs
- 1/2 cup coconut flour
- 1/2 cup coconut milk
- 1 tablespoon melted coconut oil
- ½ pinch salt
- 1/8 teaspoon baking soda
- 1/4 teaspoon lemon juice
- Coconut oil for frying

Instructions:

1) Separate the egg yolks from the egg white and beat the egg whites and beat the salt with a hand mixer. Continue whisking until stiff peaks form and set aside.
2) In another bowl mix egg yolk, coconut oil and coconut milk.
3) Add coconut flour and baking soda and lemon juice. Mix in a gentle mixture.
4) Always carefully fold the egg whites into the batter. Let the batter rest for 5 minutes.
5) Fry in coconut oil over medium or low heat for a few minutes on each side.

Nutrition information According to Keto Diet

Calories per serving: 291; Carbohydrates: 3g; Protein: 12 g; Fat: 24 g

Lemon Garlic Salmon with Asparagus

Serves: 2

Cooking Time: 20 minutes

Preparation Time: 10 minutes

Ingredients

- 2 salmon fillets
- 2 garlic cloves, minced
- Juice and zest from 1/2 lemon
- 1/8 cup grass-fed-butter
- 1 tablespoon fresh basil, minced
- 1/2 lemon, sliced
- 1 tablespoon olive oil
- Sea salt and freshly ground black pepper
- 1/2 cup Green asparagus

Instructions:

1) Preheat oven to 375 F.
2) Rinse and trim the asparagus.
3) In a large bowl, mix asparagus, 1 garlic, olive oil and season to taste.
4) Melt the butter in a saucepan over medium heat, add the garlic, the lemon peel and the lemon juice.
5) Beat until smooth and simmer for 10 to 12 minutes.
6) Season the salmon and place it on a baking tray.
7) Sprinkle the salmon fillets with the ghee sauce and cover each filet with lemon slices.
8) Place the asparagus around the salmon fillets on the baking tray and place in the oven.
9) Bake in the oven for 15 to 20 minutes.
10) Garnish with fresh basil and serve.

Nutrition information According to Keto Diet

Calories per serving: 291; Carbohydrates: 3g; Protein: 12 g; Fat: 24 g

Chicken burgers with tomato butter

Serves: 2

Cooking Time: 10 minutes

Preparation Time: 10 minutes

Ingredients

- 1 lb ground chicken
- 1 egg
- 1/2 red onion, grated or finely chopped
- 1 teaspoon kosher or ground sea salt
- ½ teaspoon ground black pepper
- 1 teaspoon dried thyme
- 1/4 cup butter, for frying

Fried cabbage

- 1 lb Napa cabbage
- 1 tablespoon grass-fed- butter
- 1 teaspoon salt
- ½ teaspoon ground black pepper

Whipped tomato butter

- 2 tablespoons butter
- 1 tablespoon tomato paste
- 1 teaspoon red wine vinegar
- sea salt and pepper to taste

Instructions:

1) Preheat oven to 220 ° F. Mix all ingredients for the patties in a bowl.
2) Shape 4 burgers and fry in butter over medium heat until golden brown and well cooked.
3) Put in the oven to keep warm.
4) Cut the cabbage with a sharp knife, a mandolin cutter or a food processor.

5) Fry the cabbage in a generous amount of butter over medium heat until it turns brown at the edges. Stir occasionally to make sure it cooks evenly. Season with salt and pepper. Reduce the heat towards the end.

6) Put all the ingredients for the tomato butter in a small bowl and mix with an electric blender. Put the chicken pies and the fried cabbage and place a tablespoon of tomato butter on top.

Nutrition information According to Keto Diet

Calories per serving: 743; Carbohydrates: 8g; Protein: 31 g; Fat:65 g

DAY TEN
Salmon filed avocado

Serves: 4

Cooking Time: 25 minutes

Preparation Time: 10 minutes

Ingredients

- 2 Avocado, seed removed
- 4 Cooked salmon fillets
- 2 Onion, finely chopped
- 1/2 cup low -crab mayonnaise
- 4 tablespoon fresh lemon juice
- salt to taste
- freshly ground black pepper to taste
- 2 tablespoon Coconut oil
- 1 tablespoon freshly chopped basil

Instructions:

1) Preheat the oven to 200 F . Place the salmon fillets on a baking tray lined with parchment paper. Sprinkle with melted coconut oil, season with salt and pepper and 1 tablespoon of fresh lemon juice. Put in the oven and bake for 20-25 minutes

2) When done, remove it from the oven and let it cool for 5 to 10 minutes. Using a fork, crush the salmon fillets and discard the skin. Mix with the finely chopped onion,

3) Add mayonnaise and fresh chopped basil.

4) Squeeze more lemon juice and season with salt and pepper to taste. Remove half the avocado and let 1/2 - 1 inch avocado. Cut the avocado into small pieces.

5) Put the chopped avocado with the salmon in the bowl and mix everything until well blended

6) Fill each avocado half with the salmon-avocado mixture, add the lemon and enjoy!

Nutrition information According to Keto Diet

Calories per serving: 463; Carbohydrates: 6.4g; Protein: 27 g; Fat:34.6 g

Chicken Stew

Serves: 2

Cooking Time: 20 minutes

Preparation Time: 10 minutes

Ingredients

- 1 lb boneless chicken breast
- 1 teaspoons garlic minced
- 2 tablespoons coconut oil
- 1 cup broccoli
- 1/2 red bell pepper
- 1 cup coconut milk
- salt and pepper
- 1 tablespoon curry powder
- 1 tablespoon fresh coriander

Instructions:

1) Cut the chicken breast into bite-sized pieces.
2) Using a clean chopping board and knife, cut broccoli and red bell pepper into small pieces.
3) Heat the coconut oil in a wok. Add the curry powder and minced garlic and let cool for a minute to release the flavors.
4) Add the chicken and season with salt and pepper. cook for about 5 minutes. Stir to make sure all pieces are golden brown and well cooked. Remove from the pan and keep warm.
5) Add the broccoli and red bell pepper to the same pan. Fry the vegetables for a few minutes over medium heat.
6) Add the coconut milk and simmer for 5-10 minutes. Season with salt and pepper. Add the fried chicken to the stew.
7) Sprinkle with finely chopped coriander.

Nutrition information According to Keto Diet

Calories per serving: 781; Carbohydrates: 9g; Protein: 33 g; Fat:68 g

Tuna salad with poached eggs

Serves: 4

Cooking Time: 20 minutes

Preparation Time: 10 minutes

Ingredients

- 8 oz. tuna in olive oil, drained
- 1 cup chopped bok choy
- 1 red onion
- 1 cup Greek Yogurt
- 2 teaspoons Dijon mustard
- 1 lemon, juice and zest
- salt and pepper
- 10 olives
- 4 oz. leafy greens or lettuce
- 4 oz. cherry tomatoes
- 4 tablespoons olive oil

Poached eggs

- 8 eggs
- 2 teaspoons salt
- 4 teaspoons white vinegar 5

Instructions:

1) Mix the tuna with the other ingredients for the salad, except lettuce and cherry tomatoes.
2) Bring the water to a boil. Add salt and vinegar. Mix the water in circles to form a whirlpool with a spoon. Break the egg one after the other into the moving water.
3) Simmer for 3 minutes and remove with a slotted spoonful of water.
4) Serve salad and eggs with your choice of fresh vegetables and some tomatoes. Sprinkle olive oil over it before serving.

Nutrition information According to Keto Diet

Calories per serving: 765; Carbohydrates: 6g; Protein: 29 g; Fat:69 g

DAY ELEVEN

Chia pudding

Serves: 2

Cooking Time: 00 minutes

Preparation Time: 10 minutes

Ingredients

- 1/4 cup coconut cream
- 1/2 cup full fat coconut milk
- 1/16 teaspoon salt
- 2 teaspoon Erythritol
- 1 teaspoons vanilla extract
- 1/2 cup chia seeds see note

Instructions:

1) Mix all ingredients in a medium bowl until they are smooth.

2) Leave for a few minutes and stir again.

3) Cover a square in the fridge until it thickens like a pudding.

Nutrition information According to Keto Diet

Calories per serving: 288; Carbohydrates: 8g; Protein: 4 g; Fat:27 g

Pork Chops

Serves: 2

Cooking Time: 00 minutes

Preparation Time: 10 minutes

Ingredients

- 2 pork chops
- 4 oz. butter, for frying
- 1 lb fresh cabbage
- salt and pepper
- 1 tablespoon dried parsley
- ½ tablespoon garlic powder
- 1 tablespoon lemon juice
- salt and pepper

Instructions:

1) Mix butter, garlic, parsley and lemon juice. Season with salt and pepper. keep aside .
2) Make small cuts in the the chops to keep them flat while frying. Season with salt and pepper.
3) Heat a pan over medium heat. Add the butter to the pan and add the chop.
4) Fry chops for about 5 minutes each side or until golden brown and cooked to perfection.
5) Remove the chops from the pan and keep them warm.
6) Use the same pan and add the cabbage . Season with salt and pepper. Simmer over medium heat for a few minutes until the cabbage have a become a little softer, but still a bit crunchy.
7) Serve pork chops and cabbage with a spoonful of garlic butter melt on top.

Nutrition information According to Keto Diet

Calories per serving: 910; Carbohydrates: 6g; Protein :54 g; Fat:73 g

Caesar Salad

Serves: 2

Cooking Time: 20 minutes

Preparation Time: 10 minutes

Ingredients

- 1 lb turkey breasts
- 1 tablespoons coconut oil
- salt and pepper
- 1 salad greens
- 4 oz. freshly grated parmesan cheese

Dressing

- 1 cup low crab mayonnaise
- 2 tablespoons Dijon mustard
- 1 lemon, zest and juice
- 4 tablespoons grated parmesan cheese
- 4 tablespoons finely chopped filets of anchovies
- salt and pepper

Instructions:

1) Mix the ingredients of dressing with a whisk or a blender. Set aside in the refrigerator.
2) Preheat the oven to 400 ° F .Place the turkey breast in a greased baking dish.
3) Season the turkey with salt and pepper and sprinkle with coconut oil. Cook the turkey in the oven for about 20 minutes or until fully cooked.
4) Mince the salad and place it on two plates as a base. Slice the turkey Finish with a generous portion of vinaigrette and a good Parmesan cheese.

Nutrition information According to Keto Diet

Calories per serving: 184; Carbohydrates: 7g; Protein :5.4 g; Fat:15.3 g

DAY TWELVE

Seafood Omelet

Serves: 4

Cooking Time: 15 minutes

Preparation Time: 10 minutes

Ingredients

- 4 tablespoons olive oil
- 10 oz. smoked salmon
- 2 red chili peppers
- 1 teaspoon garlic powder
- 1 teaspoon ground cumin
- 1 cup mayonnaise
- 2 tablespoons fresh chives or dried chives
- 12 eggs
- 4 tablespoons grass-butter
- salt and pepper to taste

Instructions:

1) mix smoked salmon in olive oil together with garlic powder, chili, , cumin seed, salt and pepper. Set aside
2) Add mayonnaise and chives to the salmon mixture.
3) Whisk the eggs together. Season with salt and pepper. Fry in a non-stick skillet with plenty of butter.
4) Add the salmon mixture when the omelet is almost ready. Fold. Lower the heat and allow to set completely. Serve immediately.

Nutrition information According to Keto Diet

Calories per serving: 874; Carbohydrates: 4g; Protein :27g; Fat: 83 g

Tofu Chicken Curry

Serves: 2

Cooking Time: 35 minutes

Preparation Time: 05 minutes

Ingredients

- 1 pounds bone-in chicken breast
- 4 ounce tofu
- 1 cup water
- 1/2 cup crushed tomatoes
- 1/4 cup heavy whipping cream
- 2 tablespoons butter
- 1/2 tablespoon olive oil
- 1 teaspoon coconut oil
- 1 ½ teaspoons garlic paste
- 1 ½ teaspoons ginger paste
- 1/2 teaspoon coriander powder
- 1/2 teaspoon garam masala
- 1/2 teaspoon salt
- 1/2 teaspoon ground black pepper
- ½ teaspoon red chili powder
- 5 sprigs cilantro

Instructions:

1) Preheat oven to 375 F.
2) Bring the chicken breast and rub with olive oil, salt and pepper to taste.
3) Put the chicken on a baking tray and cook for 25 minutes.
4) Cut the tofu into small pieces and set aside.
5) Heat a pan over medium heat and add the butter and coconut oil. Let the butter begin to brown.

6) When the butter is browned, add the ginger and garlic paste. Stirred for 2 minutes
7) Add the mashed tomato.
8) Add the coriander powder, garam masala, chili powder and salt. Mix well and simmer until the oil is up.
9) Gently mix the tofu into the sauce.
10) Add to the water and simmer for 5 minutes
11) Put the heat on medium heat, add the cream. Stir to mix.
12) Cook over low heat until it boils again.
13) Add the chicken to the sauce and mix well. Cook over low heat for at least 5 minutes.
14) Garnish with coriander and serve hot.

Nutrition information According to Keto Diet

Calories per serving: 910; Carbohydrates: 6.84g; Protein :57g; Fat: 63 g

Kale with Beef and cranberries

Serves: 2

Cooking Time: 35 minutes

Preparation Time: 05 minutes

Ingredients

- 1 oz. butter
- 1/2 lb kale
- 1/2 lb smoked beef
- 1 oz. almond cut into small pieces
- 1/4 cup frozen cranberries

Instructions:

1) Wash kale, cut and cut into large pieces. Set aside.
2) Cut beef into small pieces and fry in butter over medium heat until golden and crispy.
3) Put the kale in the pan and let it cool for a few minutes until it turns wilted.
4) Turn off the heat Add cranberries and almonds to the pan and mix. Serve immediately.

Nutrition information According to Keto Diet

Calories per serving: 749; Carbohydrates: 8 g; Protein : 14 g; Fat: 63 g

DAY THIRTEEN
Avocado Smoothie

Serves: 4

Cooking Time: 00 minutes

Preparation Time: 05 minutes

Ingredients

- 1-1/2 cups blueberries
- 2 avocados
- 3 cups soy milk
- 1 tablespoon lime juice
- 4 teaspoons Erythritol
- 1/2 cup ice more or less

Instructions:

1) Add all ingredients into blender and blend until smooth.

Nutrition information According to Keto Diet

Calories per serving: 165; Carbohydrates: 2 g; Protein : 11 g; Fat: 14 g

Salmon With Pesto And Spinach

Serves:4

Cooking Time:30 minutes

Preparation Time: 10 minutes

Ingredients

- 4 small salmon
- 16 oz fresh or frozen spinach
- 2 tablespoon coconut milk
- 4 tablespoon coconut oil
- 1 tablespoon green pesto
- freshly ground black pepper
- pinch salt or more to taste

Instructions:

1) Preheat the oven to 390 ° F. Put the salmon on a baking sheet and sprinkle with half of the coconut oil. Season with salt, pepper and pesto and put in the oven. Cook for 20-25 minutes.
2) In the meantime, prepare the creamy spinach. Wash the spinach and place in a bowl to remove excess water or dry with a paper towel.
3) Grease a pan with half of the coconut oil and heat over medium heat. Add the spinach and simmer for about 3-5 minutes, stirring. Season with salt.
4) Add coconut milk.
5) Remove the heat and reserve. Remove the salmon from the oven and let rest for 5 minutes.
6) Put the spinach with the cream in a bowl and cover with the salmon in the oven.
7) Have fun!

Nutrition information According to Keto Diet

Calories per serving: 813; Carbohydrates: 3.7 g; Protein : 34 g; Fat: 72.6 g

Sausage & Pepper Soup

Serves: 2

Cooking Time: 45 minutes

Preparation Time: 05 minutes

Ingredients

- 16 oz. Pork Sausage
- 1/2 tablespoon Coconut Oil
- 5 oz. Raw kale
- 1/2 medium Red Bell Pepper
- 1/2 can Tomatoes
- 2 cups Beef Stock
- 1/4 cup Onion chopped
- 1/2 tablespoon Chili powder
- 1/2 tablespoon Cumin
- 1 teaspoon Garlic minced
- 1/2 teaspoon Italian Seasoning
- 1 teaspoon Kosher Salt

Instructions:

1) Heat the coconut oil in a large saucepan over medium heat. Once hot, add the sausage and cook until it seared. Stir and continue cooking.

2) Cut the red bell pepper into pieces, then add to the pot and mix well. Season with salt and pepper.

3) Add tomatoes and stir again. Then add the kale and put the lid on the pot. Once withered, add the spices and broth and mix.

4) Replace the lid and cook covered for 30 minutes, reducing the heat to medium-low. Once finished, remove the lid from the pan and let it cook on low heat for 15 minutes.

Nutrition information According to Keto Diet

Calories per serving: 597.67; Carbohydrates: 6.37 g; Protein : 27.03 g; Fat: 50.25 g

DAY FOURTEEN

Fluffy Buttermilk Pancakes

Serves: 2

Cooking Time: 15 minutes

Preparation Time: 05 minutes

Ingredients

- 4 large eggs, separated
- 1 cup applesauce
- 1 cup buttermilk
- 2 teaspoons vanilla extract
- 2 tablespoons protein powder
- 1/2 cup Almond flour
- 2 teaspoons baking powder
- Dash of cinnamon
- 1 packet of Stevia
- Coconut oil for cooking

Instructions:

1) Beat the egg with a pinch of salt until soft peaks form.
2) Mix all the other ingredients in another bowl.
3) Beat the dry ingredients in another bowl.
4) Add dry ingredients to wet ingredients and mixing until well blended and make a smooth batter .
5) Preheat a non-stick pan over medium heat
6) Lightly grease the pan with coconut oil
7) Pour ¼ cup of batter into your pan and move lightly to distribute evenly.
8) Cook until bubbles are visible, turn over and cook until golden brown on the other side.

Nutrition information According to Keto Diet

Calories per serving: 422; Carbohydrates: 13g; Protein : 32 g; Fat: 19.28 g

Crispy Fried Chicken

Serves:4

Cooking Time:15 minutes

Preparation Time:05 minutes

Ingredients

- 24 ounces chicken thigh , cut in half
- 1 cup Coconut flour
- 1/2 cup shredded Parmesan cheese
- 2 eggs
- 2 teaspoons pepper
- 3 tablespoons olive oil
- 2 tablespoons coconut oil

Instructions:

1) In a bowl, add the Coconut flour, parmesan cheese and pepper.
2) Break an eggs in another bowl and mix well.
3) Dip your chicken into the egg mixture and dip it into the Coconut flour mixture. We make a double dive to make sure there is a good crust. Immerse again in the egg mixture and back into the Coconut flour.
4) Put in a saucepan your olive oil and coconut oil at medium to high heat.
5) Once the oil is hot, put the chicken inside. Do not touch it! Let it sit for a moment, almost until it has the smell of burning. We want to make sure that the crust is nice and crisp.
6) Once you smell a burn, turn it over and do the same on the other side. Once it feels burned again, you can turn it a second time.
7) Reduce the temperature to a minimum and cook the chicken on each side for 6-7 minutes
8) Let your chicken cook until it's done. I like keeping my chicken nice and moist inside, only on the pink side in the middle, but that depends on your preference.
9) Serve this with your favorite sites and enjoy it.

Nutrition information According to Keto Diet

Calories per serving: 575 ; Carbohydrates: 1.07g; Protein : 66.04 g; Fat: 32.11 g

Kale Salad

Serves: 2

Cooking Time: 10 minutes

Preparation Time: 10 minutes

Ingredients

- 6 tablespoons heavy whipping cream
- 1 tablespoon mayonnaise
- 1/2 teaspoon Dijon mustard
- 1 tablespoon coconut oil
- 1 garlic clove, minced or finely chopped
- salt and pepper
- 1 tablespoon butter
- 4 oz. kale
- 2 oz. feta cheese

Instructions:

1) Mix the cream, mayonnaise, Dijon mustard, coconut oil and garlic in a small bowl. Season with salt and pepper.
2) Rinse the kale and cut into small pieces about the size of a bite. Remove and discard the thick handle.
3) Heat a large pan and add the butter. Fry the kale quickly to make it nice. Season with salt and pepper.
4) Put in a bowl and pour the vinaigrette over it. Stir well and serve with crumbled feta cheeses.

Nutrition information According to Keto Diet

Calories per serving: 498 ; Carbohydrates: 5g; Protein : 10 g; Fat: 49 g

Recipes Of Week THREE

DAY FIFTEEN

Sausage Breakfast Sandwich

Serves: 6

Cooking Time: 15 minutes

Preparation Time: 05 minutes

Ingredients

- 12 large eggs
- 4 tablespoon Coconut Cream
- Pinch paprika
- Kosher salt
- Freshly ground black pepper
- 1 tablespoon butter
- 6 slices cheddar
- 12 frozen sausage patties, heated according to package instructions

Instructions:

1. Beat eggs, Coconut cream and paprika in a small bowl. Season with salt and pepper. Melt butter in the pan over medium heat. Pour about ⅓ eggs into the pan. Put a slice of cheese in the middle and let stand for about 1 minute. Fold the sides of the egg in the middle and cover the cheese. Remove from the pan and repeat with the remaining eggs.
2. Serve eggs between two sausage burgers

Nutrition information According to Keto Diet

Calories per serving: 333 ; Carbohydrates: 2.5g; Protein : 13 g; Fat: 21 g

Ground Beef Stir-Fry

Serves: 4

Cooking Time: 10 minutes

Preparation Time: 05 minutes

Ingredients

- 1 teaspoon coconut oil
- 1 Onion chopped
- 1/2 cup Spinach
- 1 cup cauliflower
- 1 Red Pepper
- 1 cup Ground Beef
- 1 teaspoon black Pepper
- 1 teaspoon salt

Instructions:

1. Chopping cauliflower, red bell pepper, onion and Spinach;
2. In a large pan, heat the coconut oil over medium heat and add the onions for about 1 minute;
3. Add the rest of the vegetables and cook for a further 2 minutes, often stirring;
4. Add minced meat and spices and cook for 2 minutes and reduce the heat to medium temperature.
5. Cover the pan and cook until the meat is golden brown.
6. Serve and enjoy!

Nutrition information According to Keto Diet

Calories per serving: 307 ; Carbohydrates: 5 g; Protein : 29 g; Fat: 18 g

Brussels sprouts with parmesan cheese

Serves: 2

Cooking Time: 10 minutes

Preparation Time: 05 minutes

Ingredients

- 1/4 pound brussels sprouts
- 1 tablespoon Coconut oil
- 1/2 teaspoon lemon juice
- 1/2 teaspoon dill
- 1/8 cup parmesan cheese grated
- sea salt to taste

Instructions:

1. Preheat the oven to 450 ° F .
2. Cut the Brussels sprouts and divide them in half.
3. Put into a baking dish and pour coconut oil over it. Season with salt and pepper and add dill and lemon juice .
4. Roast for 15-20 minutes in the oven or until the Brussels sprouts have taken on a nice color. Seasoning with the parmesan cheese and enjoy!

Nutrition information According to Keto Diet

Calories per serving: 236 ; Carbohydrates: 8 g; Protein : 22 g; Fat: 63 g

DAY SIXTEEN

Kale And Cheddar Scrambled Eggs

Serves: 2

Cooking Time: 10 minutes

Preparation Time: 05 minutes

Ingredients

- 4 eggs
- 1 tablespoon coconut oil
- 1 tablespoon coconut cream
- Pinch salt
- Pinch pepper
- 4 cups fresh kale
- ½ cup cheddar cheese

Instructions:

1. Collect the ingredients
2. Add eggs to a bowl.
3. Add 1 tablespoon coconut cream and salt and pepper to taste. Heat a large pan over high heat with 1 tablespoon of coconut oil
4. Add your kale once the oil has reached its point of smoke.
5. Add salt and pepper while the kale begins to sizzle, often stirring.
6. Once the kale is completely withered, reduce the heat to a low medium level and add the eggs.
7. Stir slowly as soon as the eggs have been set and add your cheese.
8. Once melted, plates and enjoy!

Nutrition information According to Keto Diet

Calories per serving: 713 ; Carbohydrates: 5.5 g; Protein : 41.95 g; Fat: 57.3 g

Stir Fried Pork with Cabbage Noodles

Serves:2

Cooking Time:20 minutes

Preparation Time:10 minutes

Ingredients

- 1/2 tablespoon coconut oil, divided
- 1 lb ground pork
- 1/2 lb shredded cabbage
- 1/2 onion, cut in half then sliced thinly
- 1 tablespoon garlic minced
- 1 teaspoon gluten free fish sauce
- 1 tablespoon dried mint
- 1/2 bunch green onions, trimmed and sliced
- 1/2 handful fresh cilantro leaves, chopped
- ½ lime, juice

Instructions:

1. Chop onions, spring onions, mint and cilantro. set aside.
2. Heat a wok or large skillet with 1/4 tablespoon of coconut oil over high heat.
3. Add the onion and soften for 1 to 2 minutes before adding half of the cabbage with half of the garlic, and fish sauce. Stir until it is soft, about 1-2 minutes, hold the movement so that it does not stick. Remove from the wok and place in a large bowl.
4. Put the remaining cabbage in the pan and repeat, sauté for 1-2 minutes. Also remove wok.
5. Use remaining coconut oil and let it warm in the wok or in the pan. Add ground pork, remaining garlic, and fish sauce. Add the mint and saute. Cook thoroughly, about 5 minutes.
6. Add the cabbage and onion mixture to the wok or pan while stirring.
7. Check the seasoning and adjust to taste, then add green onions, t and cilantro leaves. Add lime juice and mix before serving.

Nutrition information According to Keto Diet

Calories per serving: 366; Carbohydrates: 2.6 g; Protein : 18 g; Fat: 20 g

Spicy fish with butter-fried tomatoes

Serves:2

Cooking Time:20 minutes

Preparation Time:10 minutes

Ingredients

- 1 lbs white fish
- 2 tablespoons butter
- 1/2 teaspoon paprika powder
- 1/8 teaspoon ground cumin
- 1/8 teaspoon ground cinnamon
- 1/2 lb tomatoes
- 2 onion
- 2 tablespoons fresh cilantro
- salt and ground black pepper

Almond sauce

- 3 oz. Almond
- 1/4 cup light olive oil
- 2 tablespoons water
- 1/2 tablespoon lemon juice
- 1/4 teaspoon onion powder
- 1/4 teaspoon salt

Instructions:

1. Start by preparing the Almond sauce. Put the nuts with the other ingredients of the sauce, except the oil, in a blender or food processor. Blend until smooth.
2. Add the oil and puree a little more. If you want a lighter texture, add a little more water or oil.
3. Chop tomatoes and onions. Fry over medium heat until the vegetables have a nice color.
4. Add the finely chopped cilantro or another fresh or dried herb. Set aside.
5. Clean the dried fish. Mix the spices and season the fish. Fry in butter over medium heat for a few minutes on each side.

Nutrition information According to Keto Diet

Calories per serving: 770; Carbohydrates: 13 g; Protein : 43 g; Fat: 60 g

DAY SEVENTEEN

Pumpkin Pancake

Serves: 2

Cooking Time: 20 minutes

Preparation Time: 10 minutes

Ingredients

- 1/2 cup coconut flour
- 1 egg
- 1/8 cup pumpkin puree
- 1/8 cup sour cream
- 1 tablespoon coconut oil
- 1 teaspoon pumpkin pie spice
- 1/4 teaspoon baking soda
- 1/2 teaspoon cream of tartar
- ¼ teaspoon salt

Instructions:

1. Mix eggs, pumpkin, sour cream and coconut oil.
2. Mix the coconut flour, pumpkin spice, baking soda, cream of tartar and salt in another bowl.
3. Slowly add the wet ingredients to dry ingredients until everything is smooth.
4. Put a cast-iron pan on medium heat. Grease with oil.
5. Use 1/3 cup pancake mix per pancake.
6. When the pancakes start blowing up, turn around. Make sure they have browned a bit at the edges first.
7. Turnover and cook for another minute. Both sides should be browned.
8. Remove from the pan and serve hot.

Nutrition information According to Keto Diet

Calories per serving: 141.18; Carbohydrates: 3.53 g; Protein : 5 g; Fat: 12.59 g

Grilled Chicken and Spinach Pizza

Serves: 4

Cooking Time: 15 minutes

Preparation Time: 15 minutes

Ingredients

- 2 boneless skinless chicken breast, cut into pieces
- 1 tablespoon Olive oil
- 2 cloves garlic minced
- 1 cup heavy whipping cream
- 2 cups fresh spinach roughly chopped
- 1 cup part skim shredded mozzarella
- Sea salt & pepper to taste

FOR THE FATHEAD DOUGH:

- 4 oz cream cheese
- 3/4 cup shredded mozzarella
- 1 egg, beaten
- 1/4 tsp garlic powder
- 1/3 cup coconut flour

Instructions:

To make pizza dough:

1. Melt mozzarella and cream cheese in the microwave for 30 seconds at a time. Mix often.
2. In another bowl, mix the beaten egg with the coconut flour and the other ingredients.
3. Mix the cheese mixture with the flour and mix. Mix remixing! Once the consistency of the sticky dough is reached, refrigerate while preparing sauce and chicken
4. Fry the chicken in a pan over medium heat until ready.

5. Add the garlic and heavy cream of the pan and bring to a boil. Simmer when the sauce begins to thicken.
6. Stir in spinach and cook to wilt.
7. Place the dough in a circle on a pizza box with your hands. Bake at 350 for 10 minutes. The crust should be pre-cooked to contain the sauce and toppings.
8. Spread the sauce / spinach mixture over the pizza dough. Garnish with chicken and grated cheese
9. Bake for 5 minutes or until cheese has melted.

Nutrition information According to Keto Diet

Calories per serving: 687; Carbohydrates: 11.6 g; Protein : 43.2 g; Fat: 54.2 g

Wrap with tuna and egg

Serves:4

Cooking Time:15 minutes

Preparation Time:15 minutes

Ingredients

- 1/4 lb broccoli
- 3oz. shredded cheese
- 1 egg
- 1 egg white
- 1 tablespoons light olive oil
- 1/2 tablespoon dried mint
- 1/4 teaspoon ground cumin
- 1/4 teaspoon salt
- 1/8 teaspoon ground black pepper
- 1 teaspoon ground psyllium husk powder

Serving

- 2 eggs
- 1/4 lb cottage cheese
- 1/4 cup mayonnaise
- 1/4 teaspoon chili flakes
- 5 oz. tuna in olive oil
- 3 oz. kohlrabi
- 1oz. sprouts
- salt and ground black pepper, after taste

Instructions:

1. Preheat oven to 350 ° F .Divide the broccoli into small pieces and place the crumbs in a food processor.

2. Add the remaining wrap ingredients and mix in a mild mixture. Let stand for 5 to 10 minutes.
3. Spread the mixture on a baking sheet, approximately 5 mm (1/4 inch) thick, lined with baking paper.
4. Bake for 15 minutes until golden brown. Remove from the oven and place the pan face down on another piece of parchment paper.
5. Back in the oven and cook for a few minutes. Remove from the oven and cut into individual portions. Let it be cold.

Filling
6. Put the eggs in boiling water for 8 minutes. Cool in ice water to facilitate exfoliation.
7. Mix cottage cheese, mayonnaise and chili. Season with salt and pepper.
8. Finely slice or shred the kohlrabi with a sharp knife or coarse grater. Distribute all of the fillings on the wraps. Fold together and enjoy!

Nutrition information According to Keto Diet

Calories per serving: 727; Carbohydrates: 9 g; Protein : 46g; Fat: 69 g

DAY EIGHTEEN

Strawberry Crunch Smoothie

Serves: 2

Cooking Time: 00 minutes

Preparation Time: 05 minutes

Ingredients

- 1/2 cup coconut milk
- 1 cup almond milk
- 1 cup strawberries, fresh or frozen
- 1 tablespoon extra virgin coconut oil
- 1 teaspoon vanilla
- 5 drops Stevia
- 2 tablespoon chia seed

Instructions:

1. Place the coconut milk, almond milk, strawberries, extra virgin coconut oil and stevia into a blender blend until smooth.
2. Add chia seeds for a thicker smoothie consistency and pulse until smooth.

Nutrition information According to Keto Diet

Calories per serving: 275; Carbohydrates: 2.5 g; Protein : 6.5 g; Fat: 27.4 g

Easy Zucchini Beef Saute with Garlic and Cilantro

Serves:4

Cooking Time:10 minutes

Preparation Time:05 minutes

Ingredients

- 20 oz beef, sliced into 1-2 inch strips
- 2 zucchini , cut into 1-2 inch long thin strips
- 1/2 cup parsley , chopped
- 1 teaspoon garlic powder
- 4 tablespoon   coconut aminos
- coconut oil

Instructions:

1. Put 1 tablespoon of coconut oil in a pan over high heat.
2. Add the beef strips to the pan and fry for a few minutes over high heat.
3. When the beef is browned, add zucchini strips and continue to roast.
4. When the zucchini is tender, add the coconut aminos, garlic powder and parsley.
5. Sauté for a few minutes and serve immediately.

Nutrition information According to Keto Diet

Calories per serving: 500; Carbohydrates: 5 g; Protein : 31 g; Fat: 40 g

Cauliflower Tabbouleh with Halloumi cheese

Serves:4

Cooking Time:10 minutes

Preparation Time:05 minutes

Ingredients

- 7 oz. halloumi cheese
- 1/2 tablespoon coconut oil
- 3 oz. Romaine lettuce
- 2 tablespoons Almond
- salt and pepper, to taste

Low-carb tabbouleh

- 4 oz. cauliflower
- 5 cherry tomato
- 1/4 cup fresh parsley
- 2 onions
- 4 tablespoons coconut oil
- 2 tablespoons lemon juice
- ½ tablespoon dried mint
- salt and pepper, to taste

Creamy sauce

- 1/3 cup Greek yogurt
- ½ tablespoon tomato paste
- 1 teaspoon ground coriander
- ¼ teaspoon cayenne pepper
- salt, to taste

Instructions:

1. Start by mixing the ingredients for the sauce; Set aside the flavors to grow time.

2. Rinse and cut the cauliflower and rub with the thick side of a grater, or divide it into smaller florets and squeeze a food processor until it reaches the size of the rice.
3. Finely chop tomatoes and parsley. Finely chop the onion. Mix in a bowl with oil, lemon juice and spices.
4. Cut the halloumi. Brown in oil in a pan until golden brown.
5. Spread a Romaine lettuce on the serving plate. Add the Cauliflower mix. Garnish with fried Halloumi and Almonds; Serve with a generous spoonful of sauce.

Nutrition information According to Keto Diet

Calories per serving: 750; Carbohydrates: 13 g; Protein : 26 g; Fat: 66 g

DAY NINETEEN

Jalapeño Popper Egg Cups

Serves: 6

Cooking Time: 10 minutes

Preparation Time: 05 minutes

Ingredients

- 2 ounces cheddar cheese
- 1 ounces yogurt
- 2 medium jalapeño peppers, de-seeded and chopped
- 6 strips sun -dried- tomato
- 4 large eggs
- 1/4 teaspoon garlic minced
- 1 teaspoon onion ,chopped
- Salt and pepper to taste

Instructions:

1. Preheat the oven to 375F. .
2. Mix all ingredients with a hand blender (except cheddar and 1 jalapeno).
3. Grass of the muffin tin and place the sun-dried tomatoes strips on the edges.
4. Add the egg mixture to the wells of the muffin tin. Do not overfill.
5. Add the cheddar cheese on top of the roll, then a jalapeno ring. Bake at 375F for 20-25 minutes.
6. After cooking, remove from the oven to cool.

Nutrition information According to Keto Diet

Calories per serving: 157.7; Carbohydrates: 1.3 g; Protein : 9.75 g; Fat: 12.28 g

Grilled Chicken Drumsticks with Garlic Marinade

Serves:6

Cooking Time:10 minutes

Preparation Time:05 minutes

Ingredients

- 1 lb chicken drumsticks
- 1/2 cup lemon juice
- 1/2 cup coconut oil
- 3 cloves garlic, minced
- 1 teaspoon dried thyme
- 1 teaspoon dried rosemary, crushed
- 1 teaspoon salt
- 1 teaspoon ground black pepper

Instructions:

1. Beat all the ingredients in a small bowl.
2. Pour the marinade in large plastic zip bags over the chicken.
3. Let the chicken kill for at least one hour.
4. Brush excess chicken marinade while cooking

Nutrition information According to Keto Diet

Calories per serving: 316.5; Carbohydrates: 1.3 g; Protein : 9.75 g; Fat: 12.28 g

Zucchini Pasta Pesto

Serves: 4

Cooking Time: 10 minutes

Preparation Time: 05 minutes

Ingredients

- 6 zucchini (medium size, cut into spiral shape)
- 4 tablespoon Coconut oil
- 4 tablespoon shredded Parmesan Cheese
- 2 tablespoon Almond chopped
- Salt and Pepper

Instructions:

1. Cut the zucchini into thin strips.
2. Heat the coconut oil in a large wok. Sauté the zucchini strips for about 5 minutes over high heat to make them slightly crunchy. Stir well with a little salt and pepper.
3. Put the zucchini in a bowl with pasta and pour the pesto sauce generously. Garnish with Almond and Parmesan. Have fun!

Nutrition information According to Keto Diet

Calories per serving: 211; Carbohydrates: 6.9 g; Protein : 6.75 g; Fat: 18.1 g

DAY TWENTY
Brussels Sprouts Hash

Serves: 2

Cooking Time: 30 minutes

Preparation Time: 10 minutes

Ingredients

- 1/2 cup mushrooms, cut into 1" pieces
- 1/4 onion, chopped
- 1 /2 lb. brussels sprouts, trimmed and quartered
- kosher salt
- 1 tablespoon coconut oil
- Freshly ground black pepper
- 1/4 teaspoon paprika
- 1-1/2 tablespoon water
- 1 teaspoon garlic powder
- 2 large eggs

Instructions:

1. In a large pan over medium heat add 1/2 tablespoon coconut oil , allow fry mushrooms until it is crispy . Turn off the heat and transfer the mushrooms to a dishcloth filled with paper towels.
2. Put the reaming oil in the same pan on medium heat and add the onion and Brussels sprouts to the pan. Stir occasionally until the vegetables soften and turn golden brown. Season with salt, pepper and paprika flakes.
3. Add 2 tablespoons of water and cover the pan. Cook until the Brussels sprouts are tender and the water has evaporated, about 5 minutes. Put the garlic in the pan and cook until it smells for 1 minute.
4. Break an egg into each hole and season each egg with salt and pepper. Replace the lid and cook until the eggs are cooked to your taste, about 5 minutes for an egg that was just wet. Sprinkle crispy mushrooms pieces over the pan. Served hot.

Nutrition information According to Keto Diet

Calories per serving: 216; Carbohydrates: 5.6 g; Protein : 13 g; Fat: 20 g

Thai Beef Satay

Serves:2

Cooking Time:30 minutes

Preparation Time:10 minutes

Ingredients

- 1 lb Skirt steak
- 1 /2 tablespoon ginger powder
- 1/2 teaspoon turmeric
- 1/2 tablespoon cumin seed
- 1-1/2 tablespoons coconut oil
- ½ teaspoon salt

Satay sauce

- 7 oz. Almond milk
- 1 red chili pepper, deseeded and finely chopped
- 1 teaspoon garlic powder
- 2 tablespoons tamari soy sauce
- 4 tablespoons almond butter

Instructions:

1. Cut the flank steak into 1 1/2 inch strips and place in a bowl or a plastic bag.
2. Mix ginger powder , turmeric powder, cumin seed and coconut oil in a small bowl. Pour over the skirt steak and let marinate for 5-10 minutes.
3. While the skirt steak is marinating, mix the ingredients to the satay sauce in a small saucepan and bring to a boil.
4. Cook on low heat for 5-10 minutes, until the sauce has the desired consistency. Add pepper to taste and keep warm.
5. Heat a wok and sauté the skirt steak. Add salt and heat over medium heat and fry for a few more minutes until the skirt steak is cooked through.
6. Serve salsa and skirt steak with almond sauce. Cooked broccoli goes well with this dish.

Nutrition information According to Keto Diet

Calories per serving: 373; Carbohydrates: 4 g; Protein : 28 g; Fat: 27 g

Shrimp Chow Mein

Serves:2

Cooking Time:30 minutes

Preparation Time:10 minutes

Ingredients

- 1/2 teaspoon olive oil
- 1 tsp garlic, powder
- 1 tsp ginger powder
- 16 oz shrimp, peeled & deveined
- 1 medium spaghetti squash
- 1/2 cup snow peas
- 2 tablespoon tamari sauce
- 1/2 cup green onions, chopped

Instructions:

1. Preheat oven to 375° F. Cut the squash in half, bake for 40-50 minutes or until tender. Remove from oven and use a fork to shred into "noodles".
2. Mix garlic powder , ginger powder, green onions. Heat olive oil over medium heat and stir fry the mixture for about 30 seconds until it smells. Add the shrimp and cook until they are pink on both sides. Stir often so that the garlic mixture does not burn.
3. Add the snow peas mixture and simmer for 1-2 minutes until softer.
4. Add the spaghetti squash and mix until smooth. Pour the tamari sauce and mix. Try the salt and add a pinch or two if needed.
5. Serve

Nutrition information According to Keto Diet

Calories per serving: 260; Carbohydrates: 1.5 g; Protein : 46g; Fat: 25 g

DAY TWENTY ONE
Zucchini Egg Cups

Serves: 6

Cooking Time: 40 minutes

Preparation Time: 10 minutes

Ingredients

- 1 zucchini, peeled into strips
- 1/4 cup tomatoes, quartered
- 4 eggs
- 1/4 cup heavy cream
- Kosher salt
- Freshly ground black pepper
- 1/4 teaspoon dried oregano
- 1/2 tablespoon paprika
- 1/2 cup shredded cheddar

Instructions:

1. Preheat the oven to 400° and grease a muffin tin with cooking spray. Line up the inside and bottom of the muffin tin with zucchini strips to form a crust. Sprinkle in each with tomatoes.
2. In a medium bowl mix eggs, cream, oregano and paprika flakes and season with salt and pepper. Pour the egg mixture over the tomatoes and garnish with cheese.
3. Cook until the eggs are done, 30 minutes.

Nutrition information According to Keto Diet

Calories per serving: 267; Carbohydrates: 1.6 g; Protein: 11.1g; Fat: 20.7 g

Salmon Cakes

Serves:2

Cooking Time:20 minutes

Preparation Time:10 minutes

Ingredients

- 1 (14.75-oz) cans pink salmon
- 1 tablespoon chopped fresh parsley
- 1/8 cup chopped fresh dill
- 1/8 cup grated Parmesan cheese
- 2 ounces pork rinds, crushed
- 1 large egg
- 1 /2 teaspoon lemon zest
- Salt and pepper to taste
- 1/4 cup coconut flour
- 1 tablespoon coconut oil

Instructions:

1. Mix salmon ,Parsley, dill, Parmesan cheese, crushed pork rind, eggs, lemon zest and salt and pepper.
2. Form the salmon balls as you can make .
3. Put the almond flour on a plate. Lay flat salmon cookies in the palm of your hand and dip the almond flour. They are fragile, then add some flour to the salmon and then lightly tap with the fingers.
4. Preheat a pot with coconut oil. Roast the cakes on medium heat for a few minutes on each side. They should be cooked and browned when they are ready.
5. Serve two hamburgers with homemade tartar sauce and some vegetables.

Nutrition information According to Keto Diet

Calories per serving: 418; Carbohydrates: 2.63g; Protein : 46g; Fat: 25 g

Green Beans Stir-Fry Recipe

Serves:6

Cooking Time:40 minutes

Preparation Time:10 minutes

Ingredients

- 2 pound fresh green beans, stems removed
- 2 tablespoons Grass-fed- butter
- 2 tablespoons coconut oil
- 2 tablespoons grated Parmesan cheese
- 2 teaspoon garlic powder
- 1 teaspoon salt
- 1 teaspoon black pepper

Instructions:

1. Fill a large bowl with water and ice and set aside to lighten green beans
2. Bring the water to a boil in a large saucepan
3. Add the beans to the boiling water and cook for 3 to 4 minutes
4. Immediately drain the green beans and add to the ice water to cool completely.
5. While the beans are cooling, melt the butter in another pan over medium heat. Add coconut oil and garlic powder.
6. Drain the green beans and leave to rest on paper towels.
7. Once the garlic begins to sizzle, add the green beans to the pan and toss them to cover the oils.
8. Season with salt and pepper and remove from heat.

Nutrition information According to Keto Diet

Calories per serving: 221.5; Carbohydrates: 4.63 g; Protein : 3.46g; Fat: 9.16g

Recipes Of Week Week-4

DAY TWENTY TWO

Lemon Cupcakes

Serves: 6

Cooking Time: 30 minutes

Preparation Time: 05 minutes

Ingredients

- 1 cups coconut flour
- 1/2 teaspoon baking powder
- ½ teaspoon sea salt
- 1/2 cup erythritol blend
- 1 tablespoon lemon zest
- 1 tablespoon melted butter
- 1 large egg
- 1/2 cup unsweetened coconut milk
- 1 tablespoon vanilla extract
- 2 teaspoons lemon extract

Instructions:

1. Preheat the oven to 350 °F and align a cupcake pan with some paper.
2. In a large bowl, stir the coconut flour, baking powder, salt, , erythritol and the bowl until smooth.
3. Whisk the melted butter in the dry ingredients. The mixture should form coarse crumbs.
4. Add the egg and stir until incorporated. The batter will start to stick.
5. Add the coconut milk, vanilla and lemon extract and whisk until the batter is smooth.
6. Carefully fill the prepared cupcake papers until they are about 2 tablespoons filled for each cupcake.
7. Place the cupcakes in the preheated oven and bake for 30 minutes or until the cupcake bounces when pressed.
8. Let the cupcakes cool on a rack until they reach room temperature.

Nutrition information According to Keto Diet

Calories per serving: 336.67; Carbohydrates: 5.73 g; Protein : 8.91g; Fat: 30.5g

Dill Pickle Soup

Serves: 2

Cooking Time: 30 minutes

Preparation Time: 05 minutes

Ingredients

- 1/2 tablespoon avocado oil
- 1/2 teaspoon garlic powder
- 1/2 teaspoon dried parsley
- 1 Bok choy, chopped
- 1/4 small onion, chopped
- 40 grams finely chopped dill pickle
- 1/4 cup pickle juice
- 1/8 cup vegetable broth
- 1/2 cup heavy whipping cream
- ½ cup shredded cheddar cheese

Instructions:

1. Heat Avocado oil and add garlic powder in a deep pan.
2. Add the parsley, bok choy, onion and chopped dill pickle and sauté for 5 minutes.
3. Pour the pickle juice, vegetable broth and cream. Bring to a boil.
4. Stir often until the soup starts to thicken.
5. Mix your bacon pieces and cheddar cheese.
6. Serve!

Nutrition information According to Keto Diet

Calories per serving: 517.5; Carbohydrates: 3.94 g; Protein :14.9g; Fat: 49.8g

Corndogs

Serves: 2

Cooking Time: 30 minutes

Preparation Time: 05 minutes

Ingredients

- 2 Sausages
- 1 Cup coconut oil
- 1/2 Cup Coconut Meal
- 1 Egg
- 1 tablespoon Heavy Cream
- 1 teaspoon Dash Table Blend
- 1/2 teaspoon Baking Powder
- 1/4 teaspoon Turmeric
- 1/4 teaspoon Kosher Salt
- 1/8 teaspoon Cayenne Pepper

Instructions:

1. Mix coconut flour and spices.
2. Mix your egg, cream and baking soda in the mixture.
3. Heat 1½ cups of oil to 400F in a saucepan.
4. Immerse your sausages and / or hot dogs in the mix.
5. Put them in the oil, completely covered with batter
6. Fry on each side for about 2 minutes on each side.
7. Remove and rest on paper towels to remove excess grease.

Nutrition information According to Keto Diet

Calories per serving: 493.75; Carbohydrates: 4.52 g; Protein: 15.4g; Fat: 45.93g

DAY TWENTY THREE
Tuna Poke Avocado Boats

Serves: 4

Cooking Time: 30 minutes

Preparation Time: 05 minutes

Ingredients

- 1/2 pound sushi-grade tuna, diced
- 1/8 cup coconut aminos (plus more for serving)
- 1/2 tablespoon toasted coconut oil
- 1/2 cucumber, seeds removed and diced
- 1-1/2 tablespoons raw cashews, chopped
- 1/2 tablespoon black sesame seeds, for garnish (optional)
- 4 avocados, halved

Instructions:

1. Mix cubed tuna, coconut amino and toasted coconut oil in a large bowl and mix well.
2. Put in the fridge and chop cucumbers raw cashews to allow the fish to marinate.
3. Once the cucumber and nuts are chopped, put the tuna in the bowl.
4. If you do not intend to serve it immediately, cover the fish and store it in the refrigerator.
5. When done, divide the avocados in half and place a piece of fish in the hole of the lawyer.
6. Garnish with a pinch of black sesame seeds.
7. Serve

Nutrition information According to Keto Diet

Calories per serving: 242.9; Carbohydrates: 9.4 g; Protein: 11.8g; Fat: 18.7g

Eggplant gratin

Serves: 2

Cooking Time: 30 minutes

Preparation Time: 05 minutes

Ingredients

- 1 lb eggplant
- 1 onion
- 1 tablespoon olive oil, for frying
- 2 oz. feta cheese
- 1/2 tablespoon dried mint
- 1/6 cup fresh parsley, finely chopped
- 2 oz. shredded cheese
- 1/2 cup heavy whipping cream
- salt and pepper

Instructions:

1. Cut the eggplants into 1/2 inch thick slices (1 cm).
2. Apply olive oil and salt with a brush on both sides and place on parchment paper on a baking sheet. Bake at 200 ° C until golden brown.
3. Meanwhile, finely chop the onion, with a food processor
4. Fry the onion in a medium sized pan over medium heat until soft, about 5-7 minutes. Season with salt and pepper.
5. Place a layer of eggplant slices on a baking sheet, then half the onions, mint, parsley and 2/3 of the feta cheese.
6. Add one last layer of eggplant and the rest of the onion.
7. Add one last layer of eggplant and the rest of the onion.
8. Ready with feta cheese and grated cheese on top.
9. Pour cream over eggplants, cheese, onions and herbs. Place the dish in the oven at 450 ° F for 30 minutes, until the gratin is golden and the cream gushes.

Nutrition information According to Keto Diet

Calories per serving: 480; Carbohydrates: 1.4 g; Protein :16g; Fat: 38g

Chicken casserole with feta cheese and olives

Serves:2

Cooking Time:20 minutes

Preparation Time:05 minutes

Ingredients

- 1 lb chicken breasts
- 1oz. grass-fed- butter, for frying
- 1 oz. green pesto
- 1 cup heavy whipping cream
- 4 tablespoons pitted olives
- 4 oz. feta cheese, diced
- 1 teaspoon garlic powder
- salt and pepper

Instructions:

1. Preheat the oven to 400 °F.
2. Cut chicken breast into bite-sized pieces. Season with salt and pepper.
3. Add the butter in a large pan and fry the chicken pieces in batches over medium heat until golden brown.
4. Mix the pesto and the heavy cream in a bowl.
5. Put the fried chicken pieces in a casserole dish with the olives, feta and garlic powder . Add the pesto
6. Bake for 20-30 minutes until the dish becomes bubbly and tans slightly at the edges.

Nutrition information According to Keto Diet

Calories per serving: 459; Carbohydrates: 4.7 g; Protein :25.1g; Fat: 37.1g

DAY TWENTY FOUR

Fried Mac & Cheese with Rosemary

Serves: 2

Cooking Time: 20 minutes

Preparation Time: 05 minutes

Ingredients

- 1/2 medium cauliflower, rice
- 1 cup shredded cheddar cheese
- 1 large eggs
- 1 teaspoon Red chilli
- 1/2 teaspoon turmeric
- 1/2 teaspoon rosemary
- 2 tablespoons coconut oil

Instructions:

1. Make cauliflower rice in a food processor.
2. Microwave for 5 minutes.
3. Dry it by turning it in a kitchen towel or paper. They want as little moisture as possible.
4. Add the egg, add the cheese and the cauliflower spices and mix.
5. Heat coconut oil in a pan over high heat.
6. Make small burgers with the cauliflower mixture.
7. Fry on both sides.

Nutrition information According to Keto Diet

Calories per serving: 39.67; Carbohydrates: 0.96 g; Protein :2.59g; Fat: 2.7g

Chicken & Bacon Bites with Green Onion & Sage

Serves: 8

Cooking Time: 20 minutes

Preparation Time: 10 minutes

Ingredients

- 1/8 lb bacon
- 1/2 lb ground chicken
- 1/4 cup chopped green onion
- 1/2 teaspoon ground sage
- 1/2 teaspoon garlic minced

Instructions:

1. Mix the bacon slices and place in the food processor. Blend until bacon looks like minced meat, but not so much that bacon becomes a paste. Add the ground chicken, green onion, sage and minced garlic to the food processor. There should be plenty of salt in the mix,
2. Preheat the oven to 350 ° F and lay out a baking tray with parchment paper. Use a 2 tablespoons spoon to measure 8 equal parts of the meat mixture and place them on the coated baking tray. Use your hands to roll each serving into a round mini ball shape.
3. Cook the mini balls for 20 minutes and rest on the plate for 5 minutes before serving.

Nutrition information According to Keto Diet

Calories per serving: 190; Carbohydrates: 1.96 g; Protein : 9g; Fat: 9g

Tuna Salad with Capers

Serves:2

Cooking Time:20 minutes

Preparation Time:10 minutes

Ingredients

- 2 oz. tuna
- 4 tablespoons low crab mayonnaise
- 1 tablespoon sour cream
- 1/2 tablespoon capers
- 1/4 green onions, finely chopped
- 1/4 teaspoon chili flakes
- salt and pepper

Instructions:

1. Let the tuna drain.
2. Mix together all ingredients, season with salt and pepper or chili flakes.

Nutrition information According to Keto Diet

Calories per serving: 271; Carbohydrates: 1 g; Protein : 8g; Fat:26g

DAY TWENTY FIVE

Coconut Peanut Balls

Serves: 2

Cooking Time: 20 minutes

Preparation Time: 10 minutes

Ingredients

- 3 tablespoons creamy peanut butter
- 3 teaspoons unsweetened cocoa powder
- 2 ½ teaspoons Stevia
- 2 teaspoons coconut flour
- ½ cup unsweetened coconut flakes

Instructions:

1. In a bowl, mix peanut butter, cocoa powder, Stevia and coconut flour.
2. Freeze for an hour.
3. Use a small spoon out a small portion of the peanut butter mixture.
4. Put it in your coconut flakes and stir it with your hands so that the coconut covers the ball. If necessary, reshape a ball.
5. Preferably cool overnight to consolidate.

Nutrition information According to Keto Diet

Calories per serving: 35.1; Carbohydrates: 0.92g; Protein : 2g; Fat:3.19g

Chicken Wings with Creamy Broccoli

Serves: 2

Cooking Time: 45 minutes

Preparation Time: 10 minutes

Ingredients

- 1-1/2 lbs chicken wings
- 1/4 orange, juice and zest
- 2 tablespoons coconut oil
- 1 teaspoon ground ginger
- 1 teaspoon salt
- 1/8 teaspoon cayenne pepper

Creamy broccoli

- 1 lb broccoli
- 1 cup low carb mayonnaise
- 1 tablespoons chopped fresh parsley
- salt and pepper, to taste

Instructions:

1. Preheat the oven to 400 °F.
2. Mix the orange juice and the bowl with the coconut oil and spices in a small bowl. Put the chicken wings in a plastic bag and pour the marinade.
3. Give the bag a good pressure to completely cover the wings. Marinate for at least 5 minutes, preferably longer.
4. Put the wings in a layer in a greased baking dish.
5. Bake on the center shelf for about 45 minutes or until the wings are golden brown and well-cooked.
6. Meanwhile, divide the broccoli into small flowers and cook in salted water for a few minutes. It is believed that they only soften a bit, but should not lose their shape or color.
7. Filter the broccoli and let steam evaporate before adding the remaining ingredients. Serve broccoli with the baked wings.

Nutrition information According to Keto Diet

Calories per serving: 218; Carbohydrates: 3g; Protein : 6.5g; Fat:7.5g

Salmon with Pesto

Serves: 2

Cooking Time: 30 minutes

Preparation Time: 05 minutes

Ingredients

- 1 lb salmon
- 1 oz. Red pesto
- salt and pepper

Green sauce

- 1 oz. green pesto
- 8 tablespoons Greek yogurt
- salt and pepper

Instructions:

1. Place the salmon side in a greased baking dish. Spread the pesto over it and season with salt and pepper.
2. Bake at 400 ° F for about 30 minutes, or until salmon flakes off lightly with a fork.
3. In the meantime, mix the ingredients of the sauce. Pesto, and yoghurt.

Nutrition information According to Keto Diet

Calories per serving: 103; Carbohydrates: 3g; Protein : 4.9 g; Fat:9.5g

DAY TWENTY SIX

Chicken Cucumber Roll-Ups

Serves: 2

Cooking Time: 15 minutes

Preparation Time: 15 minutes

Ingredients

- 1-1/2 medium cucumbers
- 1/8 cup basil pesto
- 3 slices Mozzarella Slices, cut into ½ inch strips
- 3 oz deli smoked chicken breast, shredded
- 1/2 red bell pepper, thinly sliced into matchsticks
- 1/2 cup kale, shredded
- salt and pepper, for seasoning

Instructions:

1. Cut the cucumbers longitudinally in a mandolin in a setting of about 2 mm. If you do not have a mandolin, you can always use a vegetable peeler. Place the cucumber slices on parchment paper and dry with a paper towel.
2. Spread about 1/2 teaspoon of pesto on each cucumber, then evenly distribute the cheese, chicken, pepper and kale on each of them.
3. Sprinkle with a little salt and black pepper. Roll up and put down the seam. If you want an even more beautiful presentation, you can put a toothpick in the middle for easy snacks! Serve with pesto or a sauce of your choice

Nutrition information According to Keto Diet

Calories per serving: 52; Carbohydrates: 2.5g; Protein : 3.8 g; Fat:3g

Thai fish with Curry and Coconut

Serves:2

Cooking Time:20 minutes

Preparation Time:10 minutes

Ingredients

- cooking spray , for greasing the baking dish
- 1 lb white fish, in pieces
- salt and pepper
- 2 tablespoons grass-fed-butter
- 1 tablespoon green curry paste
- 7 oz. coconut cream
- 4 tablespoons fresh parsley, chopped
- 1/2 lb cauliflower

Instructions:

1. Preheat the oven to 400 ° F Grease a medium casserole dish with cooking spray .
2. Place the fish pieces comfortably in the casserole dish. Add plenty of salt and pepper and add a spoonful of butter to each piece of fish.
3. Mix coconut cream, green curry paste and chopped parsley in a small bowl and pour over the fish.
4. Bake for 20 minutes or until the fish is ready.
5. In the meantime, cut cauliflower into small clumps and cook for a few minutes in salted water. Serve with the fish.

Nutrition information According to Keto Diet

Calories per serving: 880; Carbohydrates: 9g; Protein : 42 g; Fat:75g

Greek salad

Serves: 2

Cooking Time: 20 minutes

Preparation Time: 10 minutes

Ingredients

- 2 medium tomatoes
- 1/2 large cucumber
- 1/2 medium red pepper
- 1 small onion
- 8 olives,
- 1 package Swiss cheese
- 1 teaspoon oregano, dried
- 2 tablespoon avocado oil
- salt, pepper

Instructions:

1. Wash and cut tomatoes.
2. Peel and cut the cucumber.
3. Cut in half, peeled and cut the red pepper. Peel and cut the red onion.
4. Put everything in a bowl and add olives, swiss cheese, oregano and sprinkle with avocado oil salt and pepper.
5. Serve

Nutrition information According to Keto Diet

Calories per serving: 323; Carbohydrates: 8 g ; Protein : 9.3 g; Fat: 27.5g

DAY TWENTY SEVEN
Brownies

Serves: 8

Cooking Time: 20 minutes

Preparation Time: 10 minutes

Ingredients
- 2 tablespoon coconut oil
- 3/4 cup Stevia
- 1/4 cup cocoa powder unsweetened
- 1 egg
- 1/4 teaspoon vanilla extract
- 1/8 teaspoon salt
- 3/8 cup coconut flour

Instructions:
1. Preheat the oven to 350 degrees Fahrenheit.
2. In a large bowl, combine coconut oil, stevia, cocoa powder, egg, vanilla extract and salt. Add the coconut flour until smooth; Do not mix too much.
3. Using a mini silicone muffin pan, divide the brownie mixture into 8 wells. Place the silicone dish on a more stable baking sheet and place both in the oven on the middle rack.
4. Bake for 15 minutes, depending on how you prefer the texture and baking of your brownies. Use the toothpick test to determine cooking and set the cooking time accordingly. Add a toothpick to the center of the brownie and, if you cover it with a wet, better cook it longer.

Nutrition information According to Keto Diet

Calories per serving: 69; Carbohydrates: 2 g ; Protein : 2 g; Fat: 6g

Cheese Meatballs

Serves: 6

Cooking Time: 20 minutes

Preparation Time: 10 minutes

Ingredients

- 4 cups Grounded pork
- 1/2 cup Cheese Mozzarella
- 6 tablespoons Parmesan cheese
- 2 teaspoon Garlic minced
- 1 teaspoon Salt
- 1 teaspoon Pepper

Instructions:

1. Cut the cheese into cubes .
2. Mix dry ingredients with minced pork meat
3. Wrap the cheese cubes in the minced pork meat
4. fry meatballs .

Nutrition information According to Keto Diet

Calories per serving: 444; Carbohydrates: 2 g ; Protein : 46 g; Fat: 28g

Roasted fennel and snow pea salad

Serves:6

Cooking Time:20 minutes

Preparation Time:05 minutes

Ingredients

- 1/2 lb fresh fennel
- 1-1/2 tablespoons coconut oil
- sea salt
- ground black pepper
- 1/2 lemon
- 1 tablespoons sunflower seeds toasted
- 1/2 oz. snow peas

Instructions:

1. Preheat the oven to 450°F .
2. Cut the fennel into small pieces . Arrange in a baking dish. Drizzle coconut oil on top. Salt and pepper to taste.
3. Cut the lemon in half and squeeze out the juice and save for something else. Cut the lemon rind into thin wedges and place around the fennel ,
4. Bake in the oven for 20 minutes or until the fennel has turned a nice golden color.
5. While the fennel is baking, place the sunflower seeds in a dry frying pan and toast over medium heat for a few minutes until browned but not burnt.
6. Mix the roasted fennel with raw shredded snow peas and the dry toasted sunflower seeds.

Nutrition information According to Keto Diet

Calories per serving: 169; Carbohydrates:2 g ; Protein : 4 g; Fat: 13g

DAY TWENTY EIGHT
Asparagus Fries with Red Pepper Aioli

Serves: 4

Cooking Time: 20 minutes

Preparation Time: 05 minutes

Ingredients

- 20 medium asparagus spears
- 1 cup shredded Parmesan cheese
- 4 tablespoons chopped parsley
- 1 teaspoon garlic minced
- 1/2 cup coconut flour
- 1 teaspoon smoked paprika
- 4 eggs
- 6 tablespoons yogurt
- 2 tablespoons finely chopped roasted red pepper

Instructions:

1. Heat the oven to 425 ° F and wash the asparagus spears. Cooked Parmesan cheese, parsley, garlic minced and pulse in a kitchen machine.
2. Add the coconut flour to the food processor and press once or twice to mix. Transfer to a medium sized court. Add the smoked paprika.
3. Beat eggs in a medium bowl until frothy. Eggs are much better at asparagus if they are well beaten. Transfer the egg to a shallow medium sized bowl.
4. First dip the asparagus in the egg mixture. Hold the spear on the Parmesan flour mixture, lightly sprinkle and spin until the asparagus is lightly covered. Make sure that the asparagus does not touch the flour mixture or that the egg is too moist and lumpy. Repeat with every spear.

5. Spread the coated asparagus well on a baking sheet and sprinkle with the remaining Parmesan. Bake until the coating begins to brown and asparagus is slightly tender, about 10 minutes.
6. In a small bowl, mix the chopped roasted red pepper and mayonnaise.
7. Cool the sauce in the refrigerator and let the flavors combine. Stir well before serving.
8. Once the asparagus fries are golden and crispy, remove them from the oven and serve them hot with the sauce!

Nutrition information According to Keto Diet

Calories per serving: 150; Carbohydrates: 1.2 g ; Protein : 10 g; Fat: 11g

Paprika Chicken with Rutabaga

Serves: 2

Cooking Time: 40 minutes

Preparation Time: 05 minutes

Ingredients

- 1lb chicken drumsticks
- 1lb rutabaga
- 2 oz. butter
- 1/2 tablespoon paprika powder
- salt and pepper, to taste
- 1/2 cup low fat yogurt

Instructions:

1. Preheat the oven to 400 °F Divide the chicken quarters and place them on a casserole dish.
2. Peel the rutabaga and cut into 2 to 3 inch pieces so that the chicken and rutabaga pieces are made at the same time.
3. Season with salt and pepper and sprinkle with paprika. Put in the casserole dish.
4. Add the butter and mix well. Bake until the chicken is cooked through, about 40 minutes. Lower the heat towards the end when the chicken or kohlrabi turns golden.
5. Serve with a generous amount of mayonnaise or yogurt.

Nutrition information According to Keto Diet

Calories per serving: 1169; Carbohydrates: 15 g ; Protein : 40 g; Fat: 103g

Red Coleslaw

Serves: 3

Cooking Time: 00 minutes

Preparation Time: 15 minutes

Ingredients

- 1/2 lb red cabbage
- 1/2 cup Greek Yogurt
- 1 teaspoon salt
- 1/8 teaspoon ground black pepper
- 2 teaspoons ground anise seeds
- 1 tablespoon whole-grain mustard

Instructions:

1. Finely crush the red cabbage with a slicer or food processor.
2. Mix with other ingredients and leave for 10 to 15 minutes before serving.

Nutrition information According to Keto Diet

Calories per serving: 356; Carbohydrates: 7 g ; Protein : 20 g; Fat: 35g

Week 1

DAY ONE

Avocado Deviled Eggs

Chicken Pasta

Stuffed cabbage casserole

DAY TWO

Cauliflower Grilled Cheese Sandwiches

yellow pepper soup

Miso Salmon

DAY THREE

Porridge

Smoke salmon with Avocado

Fried Cauliflower rice

DAY FOUR

Blueberry Muffins

Keto club salad

Lemon Fish

DAY FIVE

Chocolate Chia Pudding

Spaghetti Squash Lasagna

Sweet and Sour meatballs

DAY SIX

Egg cups

Pork Salad

cauliflower pizza

DAY SEVEN

Low-Carb Pancake

Crustless Kale Quiche

Tuna Casserole

Week-2

DAY EIGHT

Easy Parmesan Zucchini Fries

Salad Niçoise

Beef Casserole

DAY NINE

Coconut pancake

Lemon Garlic Salmon with Asparagus

chicken burgers with tomato butter

DAY TEN

Salmon filed avocado

Chicken Stew

tuna salad with poached eggs

DAY ELEVEN

Chia pudding

Pork Chops

Caesar Salad

DAY TWELVE

seafood omelet

Tofu Chicken Curry

kale with beef and cranberries

DAY THIRTEEN

Avocado Smoothie

salmon with pesto and spinach

Sausage & Pepper Soup

DAY FOURTEEN

Fluffy Buttermilk Pancakes

Crispy Fried Chicken

kale salad

Week-3

DAY FIFTEEN

Sausage Breakfast Sandwich

Ground Beef Stir-Fry

Brussels sprouts with parmesan cheese

DAY SIXTEEN

Kale And Cheddar Scrambled Eggs

Stir Fried Pork with Cabbage Noodles

Spicy fish with butter-fried tomatoes

DAY SEVENTEEN

Pumpkin Pancake

Grilled Chicken and Spinach Pizza

wrap with tuna and egg

DAY EIGHTEEN

Strawberry Crunch Smoothie

Easy Zucchini Beef Saute with Garlic and Cilantro

cauliflower tabbouleh with halloumi cheese

DAY NINETEEN

Jalapeño Popper Egg Cups

Grilled Chicken Drumsticks with Garlic Marinade

Zucchini Pasta Pesto

DAY TWENTY

Brussels Sprouts Hash

Thai Beef Satay

Shrimp Chow Mein

DAY TWENTY ONE

Zucchini Egg Cups

Salmon Cakes

Green Beans Stir-Fry Recipe

Week-4

DAY TWENTY TWO

Lemon Cupcakes

Dill Pickle Soup

Corndogs

DAY TWENTY THREE

Tuna Poke Avocado Boats

eggplant gratin

chicken casserole with feta cheese and olives

DAY TWENTY FOUR

FRIED MAC & CHEESE

Chicken & Bacon Bites with Green Onion & Sage

tuna salad with capers

DAY TWENTY FIVE

Coconut Peanut Balls

chicken wings with creamy broccoli

salmon with pesto

DAY TWENTY SIX

Chicken Cucumber Roll-Ups

Thai fish with curry and coconut

Greek salad

DAY TWENTY SEVEN

Brownies

cheese meatballs

Roasted fennel and snow pea salad

DAY TWENTY EIGHT

Asparagus Fries with Red Pepper Aioli

paprika chicken with rutabaga

Red coleslaw

Made in the USA
Middletown, DE
22 July 2019